THE WILLOUGHBY CHRONICLES

BY TED PAGE

ILLUSTRATED BY NICHOLAS WILLIAM PAGE

1. William R. (Bill) Page (1920-2011)
2. Janet Page (1920-2007)
3. Calvin Page (1948-)
4. Charles Page (1950-)
5. William R. (Nick) Page Jr. (1952-)
6. John Page (1954-)
7. Theodore (Ted) Page (1959-)
8. Holly (?)

3 SWALLYS PRESS
BOSTON

Copyright © 2017 by Ted Page
First Edition 2017
Front cover and interior illustrations by Nicholas William Page
All rights reserved

Paperback ISBN 978-0-9882300-8-8
Hardcover ISBN 978-0-9882300-9-5
E-book ISBN 978-0-9987651-0-5
1. Memoir. 2. Short Stories

3 Swallys Press
Cambridge, MA

3swallyspress.com

Acknowledgments

For years I used to try to write entertaining fictional stories, often trying a little too hard. One that stands out in my mind involved my central character waking up in a freezer case and realizing he had been reincarnated as a Carvel Ice Cream cookie whale. That story, like many others, was never published. Then my wife, Nancy, said, "Why don't you write about something *really* weird. Like your family." I took this loving advice to heart and started writing about growing up with my four older brothers, and mom and dad, in Lexington, Massachusetts, and at our summer place on Lake Willoughby in the Northeast Kingdom of Vermont. Soon, I had stories published in the *Boston Globe Magazine*, and *Boston* magazine. And ultimately, this collection. So, first and foremost, I need to thank Nancy for telling me to write the true things.

Still, most of these stories may have stayed in my

electronic drawer gathering digital dust if not for my fellow members of the Souled Out Artists group—in particular the great Anthony Martignetti, who led me on a path toward finding my voice as a storyteller. A big thanks is owed to my talented son, Nicholas, for his great illustrations, and to my witty daughter, Abigail, for her support over the years. And to my friends and colleagues who have provided endless advice and encouragement: Fred Surr, Kacy Karlen, Anna Sternoff, Chelsea Hobgood and Jim Stetson.

But of course true stories would not be good at all without great characters, and for this reason and a million others I have to thank my wonderful brothers John, Nick, Charley and Calvin, and my parents, Janet and Bill, who were both forces of nature in their own nearly unbelievable ways.

Much love to all,

Ted

February 2017

"Bring us home, brother."

—ANTHONY MARTIGNETTI

Contents

The Ledge 1

No Cartoons 5

Balloons 6

Vast and Infinitely Beautiful 10

Bobby 21

Going Up the Brook 23

Chopper 27

Mrs. Delsie 35

4-F 41

George and Big Cat 47

The Play House 50

Sex 53

The Circus 61

Catching Fireflies in a Jar 65

Nuclear Attack	68
Pay-Per-View	69
John's Machines	75
Payback	78
Hiroshima Day	80
Four Strong Winds	87
Dead Animals	90
Puppies	95
Death Molecule	105
Moving Boulders in the Brook	106
Nixon	110
Sapling Maples	111
Fourth of July	113
Digging the Hobby Hole	122
Bella	132
The Great Meadow	136
Stronger Together	141
Band	146
She Who Makes All Things Grow	150
The Pineapple	156
The Accidental Guardian	163

The Ledge

I am a baby, crying, a baby crying my head off, crawling around upstairs, into my father and mother's bedroom on the second floor of our big old brown house in Lexington. Mom is not here. Dad is by the big round mirror, fixing his tie.

Suddenly Dad opens the window and the screen, which start at floor level, and he lifts me up and sets me out on the ledge. I hear the window close behind me. I stop crying, and crawl to the end of the ledge—there is no railing—and my lips form a little "O" of wonder when I see how far down the earth is below, the brush rolling down the steep hill, the gray rocks, the trees that rise up beyond the top of the house—and in a little peek through the pretty green leaves, shiny buildings off in the distance. It's quiet here. The air smells of things growing. I make soft noises, my fingers holding the rough edge of roof as I stare out in awe.

Time passes.

Suddenly Mom opens the window and lifts me back in. She is upset for some reason, and she holds me close with my head against her shoulder and screams at Dad, "What's wrong with you! Are you trying to kill him?"

Dad turns, still fixing his tie. "Don't be ridiculous, Janet."

"Ridiculous? Are you mad? You put Teddy on the ledge! Why would you *do* such a thing?"

Dad keeps finishing with his tie as he explains, "All living things have a built-in instinct for survival. Even as a baby, the ancient, reptilian portion of Teddy's brain understands that crawling off the ledge would result in his death, so he . . ."

"Teddy's not a *reptile*!"

"I didn't say he was a reptile. What I said was that the reptilian portion of his brain, which is the oldest section in evolutionary terms, has . . ."

"I'll never trust you again!"

"Don't say that, Janet! You don't understand!"

"I understand *perfectly*! You're crazy!"

They are both talking at once as Mom stomps out of the room, and I'm crying.

"I have to get to work," Dad says. "I'll explain later."

"Don't bother!"

"You're getting hysterical over nothing, Janet!"

"Damn you to hell!"

No Cartoons

Everybody's really sad and I don't know why. I'm bored, and not old enough to read. I turn on the TV. There are men in uniforms, people crying. A coffin covered with a flag. All three channels show the same thing, which is not fair.

There's a horse with no rider. And no cartoons on.

Balloons

It's my sixth birthday party, and my oldest brother Calvin is filling a large balloon with gas from his industrial blowtorch. Calvin, 11 years older than me, looks excited as the balloon continues to grow, from nothing to about four feet wide. The idea, explains Calvin, is to attach the balloon to a long bamboo pole and hang it over a candle. A balloon with just oxygen or acetylene gas by itself would just pop. But the two gasses together will erupt into a huge fireball.

Mom is in the kitchen putting the finishing touches on my cake.

My friend Chopper and about six other friends of mine are playing tag, running in circles and laughing. The sun is out, but we're under the shade of big maple trees.

Calvin ties the full balloon to the pole and lights the candle. I'm so excited. And lucky to have a big

BALLOONS

brother who knows how to create real bombs—not like those puny firecrackers. Sometimes Calvin cuts the heads off of matches and stuffs them into lead pipes. He says you have to do it carefully so they don't blow up in your face; if they did they'd rip your whole face off. There's something about the danger that makes him really happy. Dad, who started out as a chemical engineer, has a whole chemistry lab in the basement, but I don't think Dad knows what Calvin does down there. Sometimes my brother Charley helps out with the bombs, but Charley doesn't think about the bombs in the same way as Calvin. Charley, two years younger than Calvin, likes to earn merit badges and do favors for people. He's an Eagle Scout. But Calvin just likes to blow things up.

A lot.

Calvin has straight sandy-brown hair that's neatly combed; his face is long and thoughtful. Like all of my four older brothers, he's tall—about six three. Always safety-minded, Calvin gets the attention of my friends and tells everyone to stand back. Then, with his free hand clamped over one ear, he holds the pole with the bobbing gigantic balloon over the candle.

In an instant we are smaller versions of those test-dummy GI's I've seen on TV getting blown away by nuclear bombs at Los Alamos.

The explosion is staggering. Kids are screaming and running away from the lawn. Calvin is knocked several feet back, still holding the bamboo pole, which is now frayed three feet back from the end. He laughs and says, "Holy shit!"

Mom arrives with my cake just as the police pull into the driveway. Calvin, looking kind of stunned and really happy at the same time, sees the police and quickly hauls his blowtorch into the basement.

The sight of the police has drawn my friends to the cruiser like it's the newest attraction at the party. First a nuclear bomb, now the police. This is much better than having a clown or some other stupid thing. We all gather around the policeman and look up at him as he gets out of the car. He has a real gun!

The policeman pulls up his belt and looks at my mom through his dark glasses. He says, "We got some calls about an explosion."

"An explosion?" Mom says. "I didn't hear anything."

The policeman looks at her sideways. I bet he's heard complaints from the neighbors before about this house. But maybe because there's a birthday party going on he figures nobody in their right mind would let a bomb go off around a bunch of kids. What he doesn't know is that we're not in our right minds and that's on purpose. Dad says we should always question authority because it was the authorities who started wars and were still trying to ruin the world and keep us from "becoming all we are capable of becoming," although I'm not sure what that means.

BALLOONS

The policeman takes off his hat, scratches his head, gets back in the car and drives off. Mom starts to sing the "Happy Birthday" song and everybody joins in.

Vast and Infinitely Beautiful

It's 1966 and time for us to see the great American West. Dad flew over the whole darn thing not too long ago and he says it is VAST and INFINITELY BEAUTIFUL. So we're going to go, all of us. It's going to be a really great adventure, that's what. Dad buys a van and he and Charley and Calvin make a wooden thing to put inside, a big box that can hold all of our stuff, sleeping bags and tent and cooking gear, and there's still some room in the seats, Dad says, for all of us to sit—seven of us, no problem.

"Isn't this exciting!" Mom says to me and my youngest older brother, John, over and over. "Just think what great things we're going to see."

"Indians?" John asks.

"Sure. Lots of Indians."

"Indians in teepees?" I ask.

"Oh, yes, Indians in teepees. And," Mom bends

down and hugs me, "we'll get to see one of the great Wonders of the World—the Grand Canyon!"

"Wow!" I say.

"Wow!" John says. He starts running around doing an Indian call.

The day comes for us to leave and Dad is taking lots of Polaroid pictures of us lined up by the van. He works for Polaroid so we've got a whole bunch of instant film. He unfolds the camera, snaps the shot, waits a minute, staring at his watch, then opens the back of the camera and peels out the black and white picture. I reach to take it from him, but he stops me. "Hold on, Ted, we have to coat it." He takes a wet thing out of a tube and wipes it across the picture, making it all sticky. Then he stores the picture in a box in the glove compartment before anybody can look at it, but that's OK because we're off! We are ON THE ROAD to the WEST.

I'm in the way back seats with John and we're bouncing up and down, sticking our faces to the glass.

"When are we going to see Indians?" I ask Mom.

"We're still in Massachusetts, idiot," Calvin says.

"Shh. Calvin, don't call your brother an idiot," Mom says. To me she says, "Not yet, dear."

Dad shouts from the front, "First we have to go through about ten states."

I'm not sure exactly what a state is but I'm getting a feeling it must be pretty big because we've been in the car a long time already and all I can see out the window are Howard Johnson's restaurants and gas stations. We start playing the guessing game.

"OK," Nick, my middle brother, says. "Who am I?"

"A fat moron," Calvin says.

"Oh stop, Calvin," Mom says.

John shouts, "George Washington!"

"Abraham Lincoln!" I shout.

"No, no," Nick says, "ask me if I have two legs."

Charley asks him if he has two legs.

"Yes, I do," Nick says.

Calvin says, "Are you a two-legged fat moron?"

"CALVIN!" everybody says at once. Charley knocks Calvin over the head with a pillow and now they're fighting again.

I don't know if we're in the same state we were before but there still aren't any Indians out the window and I have to pee.

"You'll have to wait," Dad says.

Mom holds up a milk bottle. "Just go in this."

I put my hand over my mouth and giggle. "I can't go in a bottle!"

"Sure you can," Mom says.

"No I can't!"

The guessing game is now getting weirder and weirder and I can't keep track anymore. I don't know if it has four legs or nine legs or if it's a mammal and if it is what's a mammal anyway and I really, really, really, really have to pee.

"Can't you hold it in?" Dad asks.

"NO I CAN'T!"

Mom holds up the milk bottle.

"Just go in the bottle," John says. "I've gone in a bottle before." Well, I think, if John's gone in a bottle, I guess I can go in a bottle. So the gas stations and Howard Johnson's are going by outside and Dad starts singing "This Land Is Your Land" and I tell Mom not to look, and John too—don't look, you better not, I'm serious—and I unzip my pants and stick my penis into the bottle and wow it feels good to pee finally when you really have to go. I'm peeing and peeing and I look down and the BOTTLE IS ALMOST FULL!

"Mom! Mom! The bottle!" I say, but it's too late. I can't stop peeing—I have to go too bad and it overflows all over me and the seat and John's saying, "Oh gross!" and Nick, Charley and Calvin are laughing and saying things like, "Baby-Teddy peed in his pants!"

All Mom says is "Woops, that's all right, I've got a towel right here."

*

We go through a lot of states before it's time for bed, way too many states if you ask me. And John and me haven't seen anything at all like an Indian. I lean my head against the glass and look out at the gas stations and Howard Johnson's. I'm so sleepy. If I make my eyes slit, the streetlights going past are like fuzzy spaceships. Dad says he's looking for a motel. Mom's mad at him. We passed one a while ago but Dad didn't like the looks of it and now Mom is saying, "Well you could have stopped an hour ago!" The fuzzy spaceships slow down and stop.

"Where are we?" Nick says, waking up in the second row of seats.

"A motel," Mom says, "finally."

It looks great to me. The sign is big and green with colorful lit-up letters. HOLIDAY INN. We tumble out of the van. I was really tired before but now I'm not. This place is exciting. I've never been to a motel before.

Inside, our room is a-mazing. There are only two beds, though—one for Mom and Dad, and one for the rest of us, which means John and me and Nick will get sleeping bags on the floor, but that's OK. It will be like camping in the Wild West. Our first campout, sort of. Calvin scouts out anything mechanical in the room and takes a close look at it. The TV, the radio, and a thing attached to the end of the bed. We gather around it.

"What is it?" Nick asks.

Calvin says, "Give me a quarter."

Charley gives him a quarter and he feeds it into the machine. Suddenly the bed starts to vibrate. We all jump on. Wow. The whole bed is vibrating! Mom and Dad are laughing now, too. What will they think of next? Calvin finds something in a drawer about Vibra-

Sleep, the easy way to fall asleep after hours of driving. We feed in quarter after quarter but we run out after an hour. We all stare at the bed. It's not vibrating. Our toy is dead. So Calvin goes out to the van and comes back in and sticks something into the machine and it starts vibrating again. Mom and Dad lie down on the bed—only one of the beds has the Vibra-Sleep so they get it. They're lying on the vibrating bed closing their eyes.

"Did you put in a quarter?" Charley asks Calvin.

"I fixed it," Calvin says. That's all he'll say. He fixed it. We take a close look and see that he's wedged a small piece of metal halfway down into the quarter slot. We go to our bedrolls and lie down. The bed is still vibrating. It's been on for a long time now. Mom and Dad can't sleep. All the vibrating is making Mom's teeth rattle. Dad keeps rolling over. Finally, Dad gets out of the bed muttering, "Darn thing." He tries to turn off the bed but whatever Calvin put in the Vibra-Sleep is not coming out. Dad curses. He looks for a plug. There isn't any. As I fall asleep on the floor, I can hear the bed humming and see Dad and Mom, sitting up, glaring at Calvin, who's already asleep on the other bed.

The next day is a long one. Mom and Dad haven't slept the whole night and they are very grouchy. Mom isn't being so nice anymore whenever someone overflows the pee bottle. Dad is staring at the road ahead; his jaw is tight. He hasn't shaved. Calvin's in a pretty good mood, though.

*

We've gone through a lot of states and now we're going to go over the ROCKY MOUNTAINS. The inside of the van is feeling kind of lived in because we've spent so much time there. The box-thing in the middle of the van is covered with scribbles and food stains. Playing cards are all over the place. Nick's into eating Slim Jims and the wrappers are stuck in every crack of the van. Nick rolls the Slim Jim meat stick with his fingers so the yellowish meat juice comes out one end and he licks it off—it's really the most disgusting thing in the world. Nick's whole face is broken out with zits and he keeps sucking out the meat juice. Calvin pokes him in the gut and says, "Piglet." Nick hates that. "Piglet!"

"Cut it out!" Nick says.

"Oink, oink!"

Nick is kind of pudgy but I don't think it's very nice of Calvin to call him names like that, and Mom says that too but a lot of good it does to tell Calvin what to do.

"Piglet. Piglet!"

Nick is bright red, really mad; he's so mad he might throw his Slim Jim at Calvin, but Dad says, "Calvin." That's all it takes. Dad doesn't even have to raise his voice. He just gets this look that says we better not do something and if we went ahead and did it there would be "consequences for our actions."

My face is stuck to the window, as usual, and by now there aren't any Howard Johnson's or gas stations in sight. The van is going up pretty steep, and as far out as I can see below us there's a green and brown valley with cattle eating. And off to one side is the edge of the mountains we're heading into. The Rocky Mountains are so big. They're bigger than anything I've ever seen.

After about an hour of going up Dad says, "Weeeeooo. Now *that's* steep."

Now all my brothers have their faces to the window. The valley is way below us, and the drop-off from the road is a cliff going straight down. It's like we're in an airplane. Mom looks out for just a second and I remember that sometimes she's afraid of heights.

"Bill, slow down," she says nervously.

Dad says, "There's no shoulder on this road."

"Bill, for God's sake, slow down."

Charley says, "Dad's not going very fast, Mom."

"Yes he is and there's no shoulder on this road. If we fall off we're all going to die. Now will you please slow down, Bill?"

"I can't go any slower," Dad says. "It's bad for the engine."

Mom is gripping the wooden box thing like it's a life raft. "Bill, let me out."

"Don't be silly, Janet. We're fine. I can't let you out."

Calvin says, "That drop-off must be half a mile. Straight down."

"Bill, let me out."

Charley says, "I bet we'd burst into flames after we flipped over a few times."

John and me bounce up and down in the way back seat. "Neat," we say, "wow."

"Bill, let me out of the damn car. Bill, let me out. Let me out of the car!"

The car is veering really close to the edge of the cliff.

Calvin says, "There isn't even a guardrail here."

Mom is really gripping the wooden box thing now. Her eyes are straight ahead on Dad. "BILL, LET ME OUT OF THE CAR!"

Now Calvin, Charley and Nick are imitating Mom: "Bill, let me out, let me out, Bill."

Mom shouts above them, "Bill, let me out right this minute—I'm serious—I can't stand it—LET ME OUT OF THE GODDAMNED CAR!!"

I think Calvin and Charley and Nick are being kind of mean to Mom, but if they're doing it I guess it's OK for me to do it, so I start saying it too. "Let me out, Bill, Bill, let me out." And everybody in the car is saying it. "Let me out, Bill, Bill, let me out, let me out." We go around a sharp corner and it feels like the wheels are over the edge of the cliff. Mom is screaming.

VAST AND INFINITELY BEAUTIFUL

*

Past the mountains now, we stop at an Indian-looking place by the side of the road. There's a guy in the store who Mom and Dad say is an Indian. He's old and wrinkly, wearing blue jeans. He doesn't look like the Indians I've seen on TV. Those Indians were mostly naked. They wore face paint and had tomahawks. Behind the store there's a teepee made of aluminum that glows white in the sun. Mom and Dad buy us cowboy hats. Five white hats. We pose for a Polaroid instant picture which Dad puts in the glove compartment right away.

We get back in the car. Calvin takes off his boot to check his bandages. Somewhere last week, Charley says, Calvin bought a gun and accidentally shot himself in the foot, but don't tell Mom, OK?

*

The Grand Canyon is only a mile or so up the road.

"How big is it?" I ask Mom.

"Oh, it's very big," Mom says.

"Have *you* ever been there?" I ask her.

"No, I never have."

We get to the tourist information center and everybody gets their white hats and we pile out of the van. John, Nick, Charley and Calvin run over to get closer to the canyon so they can see down, but Mom grabs my hand. "You stick with me," she says. Off in the distance I can just make out the edge of the canyon and some cliffs on the other side, steep red cliffs. I start to pull Mom toward the canyon. We're so far away I can't see much and I want to see more. Mom clutches my hand. "No closer," she says. Her feet are planted in the dust by the van. She won't budge, no matter how hard I pull.

All of my brothers get to ride mules down into the canyon, one of the great wonders of the wide western world. I imagine them going down, down into the VAST and INFINITELY BEAUTIFUL canyon with its crumbly clay and rattlesnakes and rushing water, and this is not fair, it's just not fair. I'm almost seven years old. I can ride a mule. I'm crying and tugging at Mom's hand the whole time. I want to see. Why can't I see?

"It's very steep," Mom says.

Bobby

It's early in the morning and I'm hungry so I go down the stairs toward the kitchen. Halfway down I hear Mom crying, "Who could do such a thing? Why? Why!" I sit on the stairs and look through the rungs. Mom is at the sink, washing her hands, and then she walks over to the stove. "Who in their right mind? I just can't believe it." There isn't anything on the stove, but she goes there anyway. "They shot Bobby. How could they shoot Bobby? Oh my God. Oh Jesus God how could they do such thing?" I go into the kitchen and try to comfort her but it's no use. Bobby is dead now, Bobby is dead. Mom is crying harder than I've ever seen her cry and it's scaring me. She keeps going to the sink, washing those hands that can't be dirty, and saying over and over, "Oh Jesus God Jesus why did they have to take Bobby, too? Wasn't it bad enough they shot his brother? Oh Jesus, oh God, what is this world coming to?"

Going Up the Brook

My cousin Sarah is a year older than me, and we're going to walk up the brook to the falls. We're at Willoughby Lake in Vermont for the whole summer because we have cottages that Gram and Gramp, my mom's parents, built for us, small red cottages with white trim and fireplaces made out of round white stones. Willoughby Lake is the best lake in the world—it's about five miles long and one mile wide, with lots of mountains around it, and streams that bubble up out of the rocks and roll down to the shore. The brook that runs by my cottage is really cold, even though it's a hot summer day. To keep our feet from getting cut on the rocks we put on old sneakers.

Sarah has long blond hair in pigtails. She has a laugh that comes from far down, and her cheeks get big dimples. She's a real Vermonter—from Windsor. I'm what they call a Flatlander, from Massachusetts. Still,

I'm kind of a Vermonter. I know all about the brook and the lake. I spend every summer here, anyway.

We start down at the beach—you have to start at the bottom of the brook or it doesn't count. Our feet splosh and slip over the rocks. Bunches of black minnows change direction like fast clock hands. Water spiders stand on tiptoe and dart away. We come to the culvert, a big metal tube that runs under the road, and we walk inside. The walls are dark and slimy and we shout and laugh just to hear how loud our voices sound. On both ends, the world outside is round and bright. Sarah slips and falls on her bum, so I slip just for the fun of it.

Then we move on. As we go up the brook, the sounds of people and cars on the road slowly fade away, and all we hear is the splash and gurgle of water, and we smell the green of moss and the sweet rot of wood. Every turn in the brook feels like an adventure, even though we've gone up to the falls many times.

Sarah stops by a big pool and leans over it, trying to catch a water spider. One of them dashes through her reflection. She's got it. Holds it up for me to see. I wonder how their feet let them stand on water.

We come to the falls, our place. The stones are many feet across and they slope just enough so you can walk on them, unless they're wet and the moss is slippery. Birch trees hang over the water and rocks. Their roots stick out, too, where the water has rushed away the dirt. Sarah and me sit on the rocks for a long time and swish our feet back and forth in the cold water.

Then we decide to do something kind of risky. We'll go higher up the brook, beyond the falls. For a while, the brook looks a lot like it does lower down. At times the climb over the wet rocks is steep. We keep going. Should we go this far without telling our parents? Sure, why not.

We come to a place like we've not seen before. It's a dam of some kind. Made of cement, about seven feet high, and water pours through a space in its center. We climb right up to the base of it. And that's when I see the dead dog. It's a small dog, a terrier maybe, lying on its side on a rock to the right of the dam. Flies are buzzing around it and clustered on its jelly-dead eyes. Its fur is matted and gross. It's really, really dead.

Sarah and I hold our noses and jump backwards, yelling "YUCK!"

Next year, when we go up the brook, we won't go this far, because this is where the dead dog is. It will always be here, even when I am an old man.

Chopper

Mom pours milk onto my Corn Flakes. "There's going to be a hurricane, Teddy. Might be a big one."

"What happens in a hurricane?"

"Oh," she says. She puts the cereal bowl in front of me. "A hurricane is a very big storm. The wind can get so strong it knocks over whole houses. When I was a girl we had a hurricane that was just awful. Awful."

"Is it like in *The Wizard of Oz* with the witch on her bicycle?"

"No, that's a tornado, but it's the same idea. Very high winds."

"Rain, too?"

"Oh yes, terrible rain." Mom sits at the kitchen table with me and unfolds the *Boston Globe* to the weather section. "Let's see now. They're predicting heavy rains and winds up to 100 miles an hour. It all depends on which way the storm wants to go. If it curves east it will just veer out past the Cape and skip us in Lexington. If it curves north we'll be right in the path."

Wow, I'm thinking. This is great. A real hurricane. "Can I go over to Chopper's house?"

Mom licks something off her lip and chuckles. "I don't think so."

"Why not? C'mon. You said yesterday I could go over and play."

She thinks for a second. "Well, the storm is supposed to hit late this afternoon. I'll let you go over this morning but you have to call me at lunchtime. If the storm starts to head this way you'll have to come home. Now listen, Teddy, if I say to come home don't dillydally. Understood?"

"OK."

I finish up my cereal and run out the door and Mom calls out to me, "And watch out for Chopper's mother! You know she's an alcoholic!"

"Sure, Mom!"

I run over the top of Meriam Hill and down the other side to Chopper's house. Chopper is my best friend in fourth grade. He was my best friend in third and second grades too, and he's always going to be my best friend. His house is huge, even bigger than mine. It has about 12 rooms that I've been in and a lot more that I've only seen the doors of.

"Chopper!" I yell when I run in the door. I come

over so much I don't have to ring the bell. I go straight into the kitchen. Chopper's mom is slumped over in a chair. Her long, straight brown-dyed hair is down over her eyes and her puffy white face. An extra-long Pall Mall cigarette sticks out from her lips and she's holding a big juice glass full of red wine.

"Choppa!" she shouts out. "Ted's here! Choppa!" Chopper says his mom named him that because she likes lamb chops. Chopper's pet skunk wanders in. As soon as the skunk sees me he turns around and lifts his tail, but it's OK because they had his smell bag taken out when they bought him. It's this totally wild animal though, and you can never pet it like a cat. All it ever does is try to get away or spray you. Chopper also has a big pet iguana. Every once in a while it gets out of its cage and runs around slashing things with its long sharp tail. Chopper had to get three stitches once. "Choppa!"

Chopper runs in. He smiles when he sees me. He's shorter than I am (everybody is) and he has a wide face and brown hair that comes down to just above his eyes. His teeth are like white pebbles. "Did ya hear about the hurricane?" he says.

"Choppa, get that damn skunk outta here, he makes me nervous," says Chopper's mom. She's slurring a lot. She waves a hand and says, "Get it out." Chopper goes to pick up his skunk but it just turns around and tries to spray him. He runs after it and it runs away. "I hate that fuckin' thing," says his mom.

Chopper's little sister, Sherry, comes in. He hates her more than anything. He keeps tying her up with the phone cord and leaving her in a closet. She's free at the moment, though, and goes into the pantry to get some cereal. Chopper's dad comes in a second later.

"Choppa," says his dad, "help me tape up the windows. This storm's going to be a doozy."

"Fuckin' storms," says his mom. "What'd they say on the weatha?"

"Could be bad," says his dad. "Better safe than sorry." Chopper's dad is pudgy and going bald but he grows his hair long on one side and combs it over. It's always half in the air though, even without any wind at all, like a half-open box. The skunk runs back in the kitchen and tries to spray everybody.

"Fuckin' skunk," says his mom. She pours herself more wine. "Why'd we ever buy that fuckin' thing?"

"Helen," says his dad, "you know you shouldn't be drinking. The doctor said..."

"Yeah, what does he know anyway? I'm just having one glass. One glass ain't gonna kill me."

Chopper looks at his mom and I can see he's sad and mad at the same time. He told me once he wished he had a mom like mine. Somebody who wasn't drunk all the time and who could actually cook dinner. I feel bad for him.

Chopper's dad shakes his head and motions for Chopper and me to follow him. Chopper's sister tries to follow us but he turns on her. "You stay away from me or I'll tie you up!"

"I'll tell Mom if you do!"

"Like that's going to do a lot of good!"

"I'll tell Dad!"

"You tell and I'll whip your ass!"

"I swear I'll tell him!"

I can see Chopper's mom in the background swilling wine.

Chopper stands over his little sister. Her curly brown hair is all over the place and she's like an insane Shirley Temple. Chopper sticks a finger in her face and hisses, "You tell and I'll tie you up so good you'll never see daylight."

His sister makes a "hmph" sound with her pursed lips and stomps off.

Outside, Chopper and me help his dad stick masking tape in big X's across the windows. There are dozens of big windows and we go through a ton of tape. We break for lunch around noon and go in to eat. Chopper's mom is sitting in the exact same position at the kitchen table. I can't tell if she's on the same bottle of wine or a new one. Chopper's dad tries to comb down the lid of his hair (it doesn't stay down) and cranks open some Campbell's tomato rice soup. We slurp it up at the table sitting next to Chopper's mom, who doesn't say anything. She's just slumped there, her hair totally covering her face. She's like Cousin Itt on

The Addam's Family. Chopper's little sister peeks in, just the top of her head, and Chopper holds up one finger and slits his eyes, warning her, and she disappears.

After lunch we go back outside to finish taping up. The wind is starting to blow now, and the long branches of the big maple and pine trees around the house are swaying. Around three o'clock Chopper's dad says we all better get inside. We run, all excited, into the living room, and Chopper's mom is walking by and suddenly she screams and points, "On your leg!"

"What!" I say, looking at my leg, terrified. "What is it?"

"A BIG BUG! IT'S CRAWLING!" Her hair is over her face, but one eye, all puffy and scared, shows through.

There's nothing on my leg. Chopper pulls at my sleeve; he's seen this before. We go up to Chopper's room way up on the top floor. There's staircase after staircase. Chopper kicks at one door on the way and hisses, "Little brat." Down a hallway we pass another room that looks like a living room of some kind and Chopper's grandmother is in there smoking a long cigarette. She owns the house, according to Chopper. She's his mom's mom. Today she's all dressed up and wearing pearls. She sits in a wingback chair. Her face is one big wrinkle and she puffs on her cigarette and looks at me coolly as we pass.

And on we go up one last staircase and down a long

CHOPPER

wood-paneled corridor to Chopper's room. It's small with a slanted ceiling, Marvel Comics posters are on the walls, clothes are all over the floor.

"Let's see what it's doing," Chopper says. So we go to the small window at the edge of his bed and lie down with our heads resting on our hands and look out at the storm. The rain is coming down slanted and hard, making little bomb crater explosions on the long hood of the Chevy in the driveway. The air looks thick. The sound of the wind rises and falls, rumbling against the window. Nothing is flying through the air yet, but the trees are going nuts. Their branches are like the evil monster robot on *Lost in Space* waving his arms up and down and saying, "Crush! Kill! Destroy! Crush! Kill! Destroy!"

Chopper says, "Awesome."

"Wow," I say.

One tree in particular is really swaying. It's the biggest tree on the lawn, a giant pine that's way taller than the house. I can just make out the top of the tree swaying in the heavy rain. Chopper looks at me. I look at Chopper. His eyes say to me, *Do you think we should?* And I look right back with my eyes saying, *Absolutely*.

We slip out past Chopper's drunk mom and run through the tropical wind and sideways rain to the base of the tree. There are plenty of branches low down—we've never gone up this tree before, but it looks like a good climbing tree. Lots to hold on to. Chopper starts up one side, I start up the other. Close to the ground the tree doesn't seem to be swaying too much and it's easygoing, although the bark is real rough and sticky and tough on my hands. We keep saying to each other, "This is fan-tastic!" We climb higher and higher. About halfway up, the tree is moving pretty good, back and forth and side to side. The wind seems like it's going every which way. Chopper's house is off to my right, getting smaller below me.

Higher we go, reaching way up for thick branches that will hold our weight. It's good to grab on with both hands and have at least one good foothold. I'll go higher than Chopper, I bet; I'm bigger after all. We're getting closer and closer together because the tree trunk is getting smaller the higher we go. I see Chopper look over at me; we're so close now we can join arms around the trunk. There aren't any branches above strong enough to hold either of us. This will have to do. We lock arms, hugging the tree. When the wind is steady, the tree just vibrates, but when the big gusts come we bend back, back, back, we're still going back, then the wind lets up. Whoosh! The tree flips in the other direction. Me and Chopper are laughing.

Mrs. Delsie

"Here, Teddy, let me show you," says Mrs. Delsie, my fourth grade teacher. She's round and little with gray hair, glasses and lots of chins. She likes me, I think. Mrs. Delsie brings a chair up to mine and takes the top off the box on my desk. Her voice is kind of pinched because her nose is usually stuffy. "It may seem hard when you first look at it, but it's actually a much better way to understand math concepts."

Math concepts. Oh no. Oh no, please. My whole body is frozen. I can handle anything but math concepts. Mrs. Delsie is very nice, though; I'll just try to calm down and she'll help me. She always helps me. The box shows row after row of rectangular colored wooden blocks. Some are shorter than others. Mrs. Delsie takes out a long blue one, a shorter yellow one and an even shorter green one. She smiles sweetly at me. I try to smile back.

"This blue block represents a blah blah. You remember blah blahs, we went over them last week. Do you remember those?"

I gulp and nod. I can't admit to her that I don't remember a thing. I didn't get it the day she talked about it and I sure don't get it now.

"And this yellow block represents a blah blah blah. You remember those—that's easy. And this little green one, what do you think this one would be?"

It looks a lot like a little green block. I can't see how it has anything to do with math. And even if it did I wouldn't want to know anything about it because I hate math. All I want to do is write. I wish she'd just let me write. I say, "A... um... an equal sign?"

Mrs. Delsie says, "Why, no. But that's such a *good* try. Actually, this one here is a blah blah blah blah. See?"

I nod. What is she talking about?

"Now, I'm going to go help one of the other children. Why don't you work for a while on your own equation. Can you do that for me?"

"Yes."

"Good."

I look up at the clock. Two more hours until school is out. What am I going to do? Chopper's across the room—Mrs. Delsie put him there after the first day because we "acted up" a little. I try to catch Chopper's eye but he's doing something with his colored blocks.

MRS. DELSIE

Maybe he knows what they are, but I doubt it. I dump out the entire box of blocks and start stacking them to make a building. My blah blahs make the foundation. The blah blah blahs are the bricks for the walls—there are lots of those—and my blah blah blah blahs are the windows. It's a really neat-looking house and I bet it means lots of things in math to somebody.

Peter Boynton is two seats down from me. He's got curly brown hair and pulls down his pants to show his penis when he's telling a joke, which he's not doing now. Now he's moving his blocks around. He sees me looking at him and whispers loudly, "Do you know what she's talking about?"

"Are you kidding?"

Peter laughs and sticks a blah blah up his nose. I can tell we are all going to be working at NASA someday.

Mrs. Delsie circles back toward me, hands behind her back, looking down to inspect equations or whatever. "Good job, Mary, very good. Paul—excellent work. That's nice, Shelly, but you might want to put your fizoodle blah snick over to the right of the blah blah blah; would you like to try that?"

Then she sees my building. "My my, Teddy, you've been very busy."

"Yes I have."

I can't tell if she's mad or just tired. She says, "And what does this represent?"

"It represents a house."

A little bit of a smile shows up on one side of her mouth. I've got her. She can't get mad at me now.

"What kind of house? A math house?"

Peter Boynton looks over at me; now he has a whole nose full of blah blahs. I don't laugh, though, because that would make Mrs. Delsie mad. "Yes," I say, "it's a math house, I guess."

"Now, Teddy." She takes off her glasses and rubs her eyes. "I know you can do this."

"Yes."

"I know if you try you can do this. Now will you try for me?"

I'd really like to try; I would do anything for Mrs. Delsie. She's warm and nice like everybody's grandmother should be. I could see her baking pies for the whole world. But math is really hard for me. I just can't do it, at least not the way everybody else does. There's always only one answer and it's never the one I come up with. In everything else, like writing and art and social studies, there can be more than one answer. I can be creative. In math, 12 plus 12 will always equal 24. But even if I follow the rules and come up with the "one" answer, it's so dull I'd rather be doing something else. I'll deliberately screw it up just so I can have some fun.

Mrs. Delsie is still looking at me.

I nod weakly.

"Good," she says. "I'll be back to check on your work."

Now what am I going to do? I look around at some

of the other kids. Paul, who always wears a bow tie, has covered his whole desk with neat little equations. Shelly, too. I'm going to be in big trouble. Well, if I'm going to go down in flames I might as well light the fire myself. So I take out some paper and start to write. The story appears in my head all at once. It's about a charming prince on a quest to become a frog so he can make a strange princess fall in love with him. She hates people but adores reptiles. I write the story in my neatest handwriting. The first letter of each paragraph is illustrated like in an old book. I laugh as I write, in my own frog world where math isn't allowed, happy.

Just as I'm finishing the last sentence I hear Mrs. Delsie above me. "How's it coming, Teddy?"

I look up at her. Her chin is pressing down on all her other chins and her gray-blue eyes are magnified by her glasses. I say softly, "Um. I don't understand the blocks. I'm really sorry. I just don't get it."

Mrs. Delsie shakes her head sadly. "I'll talk with your parents about arranging an after-school session."

"OK." I really wish Mom and Dad didn't have to get pulled into this blah blah block stuff, but what choice do I have?

"What's that you've written?" Mrs. Delsie reaches down to get the frog story.

"It's... just a story."

She takes it and looks at it briefly, folds the paper and walks off. Damn. I'll never see it again, that's for sure. Peter Boynton is stacking his blah blah blahs as high as they can go. He's got a pile that's about a foot and half in the air. Then all of a sudden the whole thing crashes to the floor.

4-F

"**Y**ou know," Mom says to Calvin casually while cutting up carrots, "you're big. You're a big guy, see, and you'll stick way out of a foxhole. You'll be like a big fat deer and those Viet Cong will mow you down in a second."

"Thanks, Mom," Calvin says. Calvin is already a sleepless mess, and Mom is not doing her best to calm him down. Calvin's Vietnam War draft number has come up and he hasn't been the same since. The news on TV keeps getting worse—the body bags being unloaded from the planes; every night Walter Cronkite telling us how many more men are dead and always finishing with "and that's the way it is." The war used to be something far off, kind of unreal, something my family protested. Now it could take Calvin from us forever. On the one hand, I think, a guy this good at making bombs could win the war pretty quick. On the other hand, this is Calvin, so things could go badly for the already screwed-up U.S. Army.

Mom just won't let up. "No matter how much you dig, they'll bag you like a buck. Boom. They'll shoot your testicles off. Imagine walking around without any testicles." Mom pokes the air with her carrot knife. Boom, boom.

Nick, who has been stuffing his mouth with a sandwich, blurts out, "Mom, c'mon!"

"It's true!" she says. "I'm not saying anything that isn't true! We're big people!"

There is a lot of truth to what she's saying. Calvin is a little shorter than my six-foot-six brothers, but still gigantic to the Vietnamese.

"I'm not trying to scare you, Calvin, I'm just saying, it will be like shooting a moose!"

Calvin's face has a hard, blank look. "I won't go."

"You have to go or they'll lock you up in jail," Mom comforts.

"I don't care. It's a stupid war. I won't go."

Mom starts to cut up some green peppers. "Why don't you get Dr. Potter to write you a note? He did that for Stevie Smith. Got him off 4-F."

"Stevie has bad asthma. I don't have asthma."

"Oh, go on. Who cares if you have asthma!"

"The doctor, for one."

I say, "Why don't you *pretend* you have asthma?"

"Shut up, Teddy," Calvin says.

4-F

At least I'm not being ignored as usual.

Mom chews a piece of pepper and plows on, "I know there must be something wrong with you. There's something wrong with everybody."

Calvin is tearing his napkin into a million pieces as he stares down at the table. "I'll eat a whole bunch of peanut butter before the exam," he says.

"What does that do?" Nick asks.

"It makes you break out in a horrible rash," Calvin says.

I'm wondering if any particular kind makes a difference, like Skippy or Jif. And if it matters whether it's super chunky or smooth.

Mom says, "Or you could starve yourself. Didn't you have a friend who starved himself?"

"Tom. But it didn't work."

"Blam, blam. You'd last about five seconds," Mom says.

A month goes by, and each day Calvin gets more and more nervous. Every night we watch the evening news and see more bloody bodies, more black bags being taken off the military planes. Calvin sees all of it. His eyes, usually a wall, are showing signs of fear—a horrible nervous fear. He jumps at little sounds. He fights over even smaller things. He is meaner to animals than usual. He's a total mess.

And Mom just keeps at him: "You'll be walking along and suddenly your legs will be blown off by a mine. Just like that." Or, "Those Viet Cong will shoot off your penis. Boom." Calvin listens to it all like some cornered animal. He doesn't want to give Mom what he thinks she wants—the joy of getting a rise out of him—but I know she's getting way under his skin.

The day of his physical arrives. Calvin leaves home in tatters. But he comes back all smiles. He apparently flunked his physical and is now "4-F" because of a rare nervous disorder that causes a rash on the skin between his fingers that will spread if he's living in a tropical climate.

Mom is delighted. And within minutes she says to Charley, next in line for the draft, "You're big too, you know. You're even bigger than Calvin. You won't even fit in a foxhole. Those Viet Cong will pick you off at 200 yards."

George and Big Cat

Mom gets two kittens. They're so much fun to play with, all you need is a piece of string or a shoelace from one of Dad's shoes or something. One of the cats is a Siamese, and we name him George because he looks like a George. We have some trouble naming the other cat, though, because he just doesn't look like a Pete or Tom or any other name. Days go by and we still can't think of a name. Then weeks pass. Months. The cat with no name is now much bigger than George, so that becomes his name. Big Cat. The name really fits, too, because Big Cat is fat. He has long black and brown hair that sheds in huge clumps all the time. If I'm in a sunny room I can see millions of cat hairs floating in the light.

They don't stay kittens for very long, maybe a month or two. And when they're older they don't get so much attention. You can't go near Big Cat without getting scratched (and covered with cat hair). And

George is good at hiding. He comes out for food but he doesn't like to be petted. The cats are just there: food eaters, couch scratchers, poopers, fur balls. Mom starts to not like them very much. We're in the middle of something in one room and she hears the sound of upholstery being mangled by cat claws and she jumps up and shouts "Stop that!" This happens 50 times a day. The cats stop for a few seconds, not even bothering to untangle their long claws from the arm of the chair or sofa, and when Mom sits back down again they go back to scratching. It drives Mom crazy.

One week it dawns on me that I haven't seen George or Big Cat in some time. I say to Mom, "Where are George and Big Cat?" She won't say. I ask Nick and John and Charley, "Have you seen George and Big Cat?" They haven't. So I ask Calvin.

Calvin says with a totally straight face, "Mom asked me to get rid of them."

"What!" I scream. "What are you talking about!"

"I shot them with my shotgun. Blam, blam." He chuckles when he says this. With Calvin, you never know when he's pulling your leg, but he does have a shotgun and he didn't like the cats.

I confront Mom: "Did you tell Calvin to go and shoot the cats?"

She's busy stirring a large pot of spaghetti sauce. "You're going to like what I've made for dinner," she says, not looking me in the eye. I ask her again. She won't answer.

I ask Charley. He says, "I wouldn't put it past him." I ask Nick and John, too. They're sure Calvin did it.

I keep asking Calvin what he *really* did with the cats. He'd say, "Blam" and smirk. But after a while he just keeps reading his *Popular Mechanics* and ignoring me.

The Play House

Behind our big house is the Play House. It's kind of run-down, like maybe it used to be the playhouse for some kid who's 50 years old now or something. It's about ten feet long and six feet wide, with green paint that's peeling. There are two windows in front, with no glass—there probably never was glass. It could have made a great place to sell lemonade, except since it's way in the backyard looking out over shrubby trees, nobody would ever go there. Inside, the floor is worn-out linoleum. I don't play here very much.

Today is Saturday and everyone in the family is out in the yard doing something useful, or not useful. Dad is fiddling with old storm windows, trying to get the screws on. Nick is on the swing. Charley is raking. John is putting rocks on a pile. I've just come out of the Play House and I'm waiting to go on the swing, but Nick is hogging it.

THE PLAY HOUSE

And Calvin... I don't know where Calvin is.

Mom calls out from the kitchen door—lunch is ready. "Everybody come in now!"

John and me are the first to sit at the kitchen table, but we can't grab a sandwich until everyone is sitting down. Dad sits next to me. He's wearing a T-shirt that's soaked through with sweat and yuck. Nick, Charley and Calvin come in at the same time, arguing about something.

Calvin says, "That's because you're an idiot."

"It's because there wasn't enough gas in the tank," Charley says.

"I just put gas in," Nick says.

"Stupid," Calvin says.

Mom says, "Boys, sit down and eat."

The argument goes on—they're always at each other's throats about something. John and me, the youngest, we don't care. It's all a show. Better to get the food while it's still there.

Suddenly, there's a terrific explosion and the whole house shakes so hard I can feel it in my guts. The argument stops. Everything stops. We are still. And then, all together, we look at Calvin.

There it is—the smirk. He's looking down at his plate, as if he's thinking about having another bite of his sandwich, but we all know what's on his mind.

Dad says, "Calvin?"

All the brothers except Calvin rush outside. Smoke

is still rising from the Play House. *Wow*, I think, *wow*. I run down to it and find a huge hole in the side. *Wow*.

We find out later that Calvin made a bomb with a lead pipe stuffed with match heads. His timing device was the usual—the head of a parking meter from downtown.

Sex

Chopper and I are fixing ourselves lunch in his kitchen and his mom is over by the table with her hair up in huge curlers. She's putting the last curler in place and I have to admit it looks wicked funny.

"Cream of mushroom or vegetable beef?" Chopper asks.

"Um, what do you want to have?"

"I like the beef."

"Let's have the beef, then."

"Ted. We can have the mushroom if you want." He holds up the can and smiles with his nubby teeth. "I know you like the mushroom."

"I like the beef, too, though."

He laughs at me for no reason I can figure out.

"What?"

"You're so fuckin' funny."

"I didn't say anything."

"You just had that look though."

Chopper pours the soup. His dad strolls in from the other room, combing the hair lid over his bald spot. "Hey Choppa."

"Hey Dad."

His dad walks out and I can hear the Chevy rev in the driveway. Chopper turns on the burner. I look over at his mom. Her hands are on her head fiddling with the last curler; she can't get it on for some reason. She's like a dancer from a tropical island in *National Geographic*—and I bet she's drunk. I bet.

"Fuckin' thing," she says. A Pall Mall sticks way out of her mouth. Chopper narrows his eyes at her. "Why don't you go to a beauty parlor and get it done right?"

"What do they know, huh?" his mom sneers. She puffs on the cigarette and blows out a ton of smoke. "Costs a fortune. And for what? You don't know nothin'." One long strand of hair has come loose from a curler and it's drooped over the side of her face.

Chopper stirs the soup and whispers to me, "I know a lot more than she does."

His mom adjusts the height of a domed hair perm machine behind her chair. She sways. The car in the driveway pulls out with a clanking roar. Chopper's mom is looking for something on the floor.

"Choppa, have you seen the extension cord that was here?"

Chopper freezes. He looks at me sideways. "No,

SEX

Mom."

"Fuckin' thing. It was here last night. Where'd it go?" She's getting down on all fours to look for it. "It can't just walk off, you know, it's got to fuckin' be here."

Chopper turns the soup off and whispers to me, "Let's go outside."

"But the soup's ready. I'm hungry."

"Where's the fuckin' extension cord when I need it?"

Chopper pulls me on the arm and puts a finger over his mouth, *shhh*. We go outside. He says, "Sorry. We can eat later."

"What's your problem?"

Chopper heads into the garage to get something to play with. He grins and says, "I tied up my sister."

"You what!"

"I tied her up with the extension cord. She's in the closet."

"You are totally insane."

"She deserves it, the brat." Chopper rummages through a stack of baseball bats, balls, a croquet set. "Do you know what she did to me the other day? She came into my room and *took a comic book*." He says this like he still can't believe it. I can hear his mother's muffled swearing coming from the house.

"So you tied her up with an extension cord? What if she dies?"

"That's too much to wish for. Here," he says, handing me a wooden sword. "You be the monster and I'll be the knight who slays you."

"Oh, that's fair."

Chopper gets his own wooden sword and we each get a garbage can lid shield. We go out into the middle of the driveway and start hitting each other.

"Kill the monster!" Chopper screams. He's much shorter than me but he's got a great swing with the sword. It comes down fast toward my head; I duck to the side and hold up my shield. I bash back. I guess I could hit him on his body if I wanted to but I'd rather not put him in the hospital. Chopper doesn't seem to care, though. He keeps trying to hit me. I duck, I stab, I bash his shield, and then he spins around real fast and whacks me hard on my knee cap.

"Aow! That kills!" I shout. I'm dancing around holding my knee. "You jerk!"

"I didn't hit you that hard!"

"Yes you did, you little jerk!"

"Did not!"

I start shoving him. He shoves back.

"Yes you did, it's bleeding!"

"Where!"

"Inside my jeans!"

"Yeah, what do *you* know!"

"You're not supposed to hit for real!"

"You don't know anything!" Chopper yells.

SEX

"Yes I do!" I shove him so hard he falls over. Now he knows who's boss. And he can't do anything about it. I'm a foot taller. He looks up at me, hurt and mad, and shouts, "I bet you don't even know the facts of life!"

I think for a second. I have no idea what he's talking about. "Of course I do."

"No you don't!"

"Yes I do!"

"OK," Chopper says, "then what are they?"

I have to think on my feet now; let's see, it has to have something to do with all that stuff Dad always talks about. I say, "It's about science."

Chopper laughs, "Oh yeah? What kind of science?"

"Um. Lichen and stuff."

Chopper laughs really hard and points a finger at me. "You don't even know the facts of life."

I am so mad at Chopper. I am soooo mad. "I'm not going to play with you anymore!"

"I don't want to play with you either!" Chopper shouts back.

"Fine. I don't even want to be your friend!"

Chopper sneers as he walks toward his house, "You're an idiot!"

"You're stupid!" I'm walking up the hill backwards. "A stupid, stupid moron!"

"Oh yeah, well if I'm a moron how come I know the facts of life and you don't?" These are the last words he says before he ducks into his house—he had to have the last word. God it's such a pain to have a best friend.

*

I'm all dirty from playing the monster and fighting and I'm wicked pissed at Chopper. Who does he think he is? The facts of life. That's ridiculous. I clomp into the house and grab a glass of milk.

Mom calls from the TV room, "Teddy?"

"Hi!"

"Why are you back already? Weren't you going to play today?"

I drink half the glass on the way to the TV room. Mom's sitting at the sewing machine she's set up in back of the room. She's making a Mod Squad Mom-dress with big yellow flowers on it. She takes one look at me.

"Well, what happened to you?"

"Me and Chopper got into a fight. He's such a jerk sometimes."

Mom sews a stitch by hand with a needle and thimble. "Oh that's what having friends is like. It will pass."

"He's so . . . I don't know."

"What were you fighting about?"

"He said he knew the facts of life and I didn't. He's soooo stupid."

SEX

Mom pauses for a second. She looks up at me, then back at her sewing. "Didn't your father ever tell you about the facts of life?"

"Mom, what are you talking about! What in the world are the facts of life?"

"It's sex, silly. It's perfectly natural. The man's penis gets all hard and he sticks it up into the woman's vagina." Mom does a quick illustration with her needle and thimble.

"Oh come on, that's ridiculous," I tell her. She's pulling my leg again.

"No, no, that's how it works. He sticks it up, see, and he leaves his seed there and that's how women get pregnant."

"You have got to be kidding me. That's disgusting."

Mom laughs. "I'm not kidding you. Why won't you believe me?"

"Because it's... it's... that can't be true." I wish Mom would get serious sometimes.

"Well how do you think babies come? Storks?"

"I don't know."

"He sticks his thing up there."

"Will you cut it out already!"

"I'm just trying to tell you, that's how it works. Those are the facts of life. Believe me, I did it plenty. Five kids. I've done my duty."

I whack my forehead with my palm and head back to the kitchen. Part of me is embarrassed and part of me is mad. And another part of me is all of a sudden realizing that Mom has told the truth. The needle, the thimble—that's where we all came from. The whole world. Everybody. Man, I'm going to tell Chopper. I'll tell him I knew all along and I bet he doesn't really know. He said he knew but he faked it to make me look stupid. He'll see who's smart and who isn't. Yeah.

The Circus

The ads for the *Ringling Bros. and Barnum & Bailey Circus* blare on the TV. Elephants. Clowns. Jugglers. It looks really fun. Besides, I've never been to the circus. And Mom or Dad should take me. After all, I'm 11 years old. It's about time.

"Dad," I say, meekly approaching the throne-like chair in his office, high on the third floor of our house. "Dad, will you take me to the circus?"

He looks distracted. The black rims of his glasses cover his eyes. "Circus!" he says. He keeps scribbling notes. I glance at the wall in front of his chair—it's a chalkboard, also covered with his notes in capital letters. One list shows 10 GREAT GOALS FOR HUMANITY to help us become ALL WE ARE CAPABLE OF BECOMING.

"Yes. It's Ringling Brothers. You know, magic acts and stuff."

"The circus." He thinks for a few more moments, then looks up. "I'll check my calendar."

A week later, I find one of his three-by-four-inch notes outside my bedroom door. He leaves these little notes everywhere around the house to remind himself of one thing or another, like dropping off shirts at the cleaners. This one reads: "TED. CIRCUS. SATURDAY OCTOBER 23."

All right! I'm really looking forward to this. I tell Chopper and he's jealous. He went last year with his dad and it was wicked.

The day arrives. It's raining. Piles of wet leaves are clumped on the lawn. Dad gets me into the car, a red Plymouth Valiant, and we head into Boston. He's wearing a dark suit, thin tie, white shirt and a heavy gray overcoat. Every few seconds he takes a stack of notes out of his shirt pocket and shuffles through them until he finds one that reminds him of what he wants to talk with me about.

"How is school going, Ted?"

"OK, I guess."

"Good. And... what would you say your favorite class is?"

"I like English because I get to write stuff."

"Good. That's good."

We get to this place where the circus is supposed to be. It's not what I expected (a great big top tent, banners in the wind, that kind of stuff). This is a big

THE CIRCUS

brick building. There are crowds of people pushing each other to get in. Dad takes my hand and pushes through the ticket area into the huge hall. I'm starting to get excited now. This is it. The circus.

From our seats, about 40 rows up, I can see the three big rings, giant circles with all kinds of wild animals and their trainers getting ready for their acts. Three white horses draped in glittering saddles prance around a beautiful lady wearing a shimmering white bathing suit and a sparkling crown of feathers. Trapeze artists are warming up, stretching their legs and waving to the crowd. Dad buys me a pack of Raisinets.

"I have to go to a meeting," Dad says, "but I'll be back. You'll be OK, won't you?"

I'm too stunned to answer. Before I can open my mouth, he's buttoned up his overcoat and walked away. I can't believe this is happening, but if I complain Dad will just get mad at me, and that would be worse than being alone. He leaves.

A clown with sad-face makeup stops a few rows ahead of me and hands out flowers to some little kids. He droops his lips, exaggerating the downward curve of the white paint around his mouth. He looks like an old guy. I wonder if he really is sad, if he hates this job. Or if he's happy handing out flowers to kids all day and doing dumb tricks. Down in the center ring, the woman in the tight white outfit is standing on a galloping white horse. A white light follows her around.

Her big smile seems as forced as the clown's frown. A bunch of other acts do their thing, then leave. Hours go by.

Close to the end of the show, I drop my Raisinets. They fall down three feet or so beneath the bleacher seat. A man with black greasy hair notices me trying to reach the candy, but turns his head away. I've never felt so damn sorry for myself.

I start to cry when I see Dad approach. People are leaving already, and I've got one arm reaching below the seat, still trying to get the candy.

Dad is pissed that I'm crying. "Oh, come on," he says.

On the way back in the car we don't say much.

A few days later I see a note that Dad has written to himself as another reminder. It's on top of a stack of other notes next to the hairbrush on his bureau. It says, "LOVE TED."

Catching Fireflies in a Jar

When I walk out of the cottage I look up at the stars and my eyes go wide. There are so many of them, so thick. There is no moon tonight so I can see every single star, from one end of the sky to the other, except right through the middle is a wide wavy band of cloud. "Look," I say to John, "look at them all."

John looks up and says, "Wow."

"Wow," I say too, "wow."

John says, "That thick part in the middle, that's the Milky Way. It's like a cloud, see? All milky."

I look more closely at the jaggy cloud and I can see that John's right. Like a picture in the newspaper, the harder I look the more I can see the little points that make up the whole thing. It's amazing that there could be so many points, a cloud of stars. My toes are cool in the grass.

Sarah runs up. "Are you ready? Do you have

something to hold them in?"

I check the lid on my mayonnaise jar. It has holes punched in the top. "Yeah, let's go!"

John, Sarah and I run up the road to the field as fast as we can, and when we get there I have to stop again and just look. The sky is full of stars right down to the edge of trees at the far end of the field, a band of black. And below, there is the shaded green-black of the meadow and there are stars there too, blinking on and off: fireflies. Hundreds of fireflies. Each one blinks on and makes a short streak of bright golden white in the dark, then disappears. There. Not there. There. Not there.

I stare in awe at the sight for a minute, then follow John and Sarah running into the field.

"Got one!" John yells.

"Me too!" shouts Sarah.

There's one right in front of me. I chase after it, but it's gone. You have to kind of anticipate where it's going to fly after it blinks off. There it is! I leap with the jar, my arms way up, and the firefly is a streak against the starry sky; then he's in my jar and I flip the top on.

"I got one! I got one!" I shout. I stare in at my firefly. His little wings flap out and his light glows on and off. Here, out of the sky, I have tamed his magic. It's not a sky streak anymore, but a fun-looking bug. I need more, though, a lot more. I run, my hand holding the top of the jar, ready to flip it open at just the right second to catch the fireflies. The only sound is the rustle of grass against my legs, my breathing, and Sarah and John shouting now and then, "Got another!"

Soon I have 15 fireflies. I bet that's more than John has. Maybe even more than Sarah. We three meet in the middle of the field to compare. We hold our jars close together and they form a lantern that makes our faces glow.

"I have the most," John says, and he's right. He's got at least 20. Well, he's bigger than me and Sarah. He can run faster.

"Wow, John, that's really great," Sarah says. "How did you catch so many?" Sarah never cares if someone does better than her; that's just the way she is. John won't tell his secret, though. He just stares down at our lantern and I can see a small smile of satisfaction on his face.

"What should we do with them?" I ask.

John unscrews his jar top. "We have to let them go."

"Yeah," says Sarah. "That way we can catch them again tomorrow night."

We shake our jars upside down and one by one, the stars scatter over the dark long grass.

Nuclear Attack

The whole family is sitting around the kitchen table eating dinner. All seven of us: Mom, Dad and five brothers. The lights go out. They're out across the street, too, and as far as we can see around the neighborhood.

"What's going on?" John asks.

"We're under nuclear attack," Dad tells us. He gets out the Coleman lantern and we finish dinner.

Pay-Per-View

Star Trek is really great. I huddle in the TV room with my brothers and stare at the black and white screen. There's never been anything like this. Kirk and Spock and McCoy, they're so far beyond the characters on *Gilligan's Island* or *I Dream of Jeannie* or any of those dumb westerns. This is outer space, the FINAL FRONTIER, and it's all so alien and wonderful I feel like I'm watching real magic shining out of a magic box.

Dad comes by occasionally, standing in the doorway, one hand on the knob. He squints at the screen, and after five minutes says darkly, "You're not majoring in television," and I say, "It's almost over," and he scowls and closes the door slowly.

Then, one day, Calvin comes home with the head of a parking meter he's stolen from downtown. He disappears into the basement, and comes out with a large wooden box. He places the contraption like a hood over the family TV. There's a slot on the side for coins, and the front of the box frames the TV screen so the knobs stick out.

Calvin explains that our TV is now "pay-per-view."

"What's that mean?" I ask him.

"You have to put money in when you want to watch something."

"What!"

Calvin chuckles snidely.

Dad is delighted, Mom is amused, and me and my other brothers are pissed. How come Calvin gets to collect money just because we want to watch TV?

Dad says, "Because Calvin invented it and this is his reward for thinking creatively. You put the money in and you are rewarded with television viewing. Calvin, in turn, is rewarded not only for television viewing but with money." Dad's been reading a lot of psychology books by a guy named B. F. Skinner. He keeps trying to tell me about Skinner but I have no idea what he's talking about, and I have a feeling Skinner has something to do with his thoughts about the pay-per-view contraption.

Anyway, it's time for *Star Trek*. Charley and Nick and John and me go into the TV room and stare at the TV with its big wooden pay-per-view thing on it. Nobody wants to be the one to put the money in. That would be giving Calvin what he wants.

"You know," Nick says, shaking his head, arms

PAY-PER-VIEW

folded, "Calvin doesn't care about the money."

"Exactly!" Charley says, throwing his arms out in front of him. "He just wants to make us grovel! He gets a kick out of that!"

"Isn't it on yet?" I ask.

John, next to me on the couch, sighs. "Yeah, it's on. The opening credits, anyway."

We all stare at the dark TV. Charley jingles some change in his pocket angrily. Then Calvin saunters in and sits in a chair in the corner. He says, "Don't you want to watch *Star Trek*? Put a quarter in."

"You put a goddamned quarter in!" Charley shouts at him.

"Yeah," Nick says, pouting. "You made the machine."

"I don't want to put a quarter in," Calvin says, playing with us. "But if you really, really want to watch *Star Trek* I think *somebody* has to put a quarter in."

Nick, frowning, pulls a Slim Jim from his grease-stained shirt pocket and nibbles the end sullenly. John—who likes *Star Trek* more than anybody—says to Charley, "Can you put a quarter in, Charley?"

Calvin chuckles, sits back and folds his arms. "Feed it. It wants to be fed."

Charley bolts up from his chair. "You're a jerk," he says, then puts a quarter in the slot and turns on the TV. John and I applaud, "Yeah, Charley!"

Calvin is positively gleeful but he's trying to

contain himself. He says almost to himself, "Amazing. Like a lab rat."

Captain Kirk and Spock are staring at some huge object on their screen, a glowing spiky globe.

"Analysis, Mr. Spock," Kirk says.

"Sensors show life readings."

"What kind?"

"Unclear."

"Damn it, Spock, I need answers!"

Uhura, the black communications lady with the big breasts, says, "Captain, we're being hailed."

"On screen."

This part is scary. An alien comes on with a long face and strange eyes, and its head is all wavy and blurry. The alien basically says that the Enterprise is going to be destroyed and there's nothing they can do about it. A commercial comes on, then another, then another. Nick is licking his Slim Jim but aside from that, everyone in the room is still. Dad sticks his head in briefly and smiles at the pay-per-view, then leaves.

Soon the show is reaching the climax. Kirk can't do anything to stop the alien; he can't steer clear in Warp Drive, and phasers are worthless. Nick asks, "Why doesn't he use photon torpedoes?"

"Shut up, piglet," Calvin says.

"Don't call me piglet!"

Kirk says, "Arm photon torpedoes!"

"I told you he should use photon torpedoes," Nick

says.

Charley shouts, "I can't hear anything! Will you guys shut up already!"

The torpedoes don't do anything.

Calvin says, "See."

Kirk and Spock talk between themselves. "Spock, what do I do? I can't lose the ship."

Spock says, "In the game of chess, when one has no more options, there is checkmate. Game over."

There's a pause. Then Kirk says, "Not chess, Mr. Spock. Poker."

Kirk opens a hailing frequency and tells the bad alien that there's a substance aboard the ship called Corbomite, a powerful explosive that's designed to destroy an area about the size of a galaxy if the ship is attacked.

"Great bluff!" Charley says.

John says, "Wow. Poker. But will it work?"

The alien hesitates. This is incredible. I love it when Kirk does this. I wonder if...

The TV shuts off without anyone touching it. We all groan, except for Charley, who jumps up and shouts, "What happened!" He fiddles with the controls.

Calvin says, "It wants to be fed. You have to feed it."

"I already put in a quarter."

Calvin smirks. "A quarter lasts 20 minutes."

I say, "But it's a half-hour show."

Calvin chuckles. "Exactly."

Charley is furious. "That's not fair!"

"I think it's perfectly fair," Calvin says grandly. "Put in another quarter and you can watch the end of the show. It's capitalism."

"It's extortion!"

Nick sighs and says diplomatically, "Calvin. Please make it work."

"Piglet."

Charley looks like he wants to hit Calvin. "*You* put in a quarter!"

"I like the show, but I don't like it that much. If you really want to watch it, I suggest you feed the machine."

We all throw up our arms. Nick runs out of the room and comes back with a quarter and feeds it in and the TV comes to life just as the Enterprise zooms out into space with the closing credits. We'll never know what happened with the Corbomite and the alien. I'm mad, but part of me has to admire Calvin's invention. It's kind of funny, even if it is evil and cruel.

The pay-per-view breaks within two weeks. Or someone broke it. I don't know which.

John's Machines

"**M**om," John says, "do we need this clock?" He holds up the old wooden clock to her.

Mom is sewing. She says, "Does it still work?"

"Yes."

"Then I don't think we should throw it away."

"I'm not going to throw it away. I'm going to see how it works."

"Oh," Mom says. "Go right ahead, John."

I watch John take the clock into the living room and lay it down on some newspapers like it's a puppy that hasn't been toilet trained. John is in junior high and he likes machines. His black hair is in a morning tangle. I sit beside him on the floor and hold my knees up to my chest. John unscrews the back of the clock and looks in.

"Ah, I see," John says.

"What?" I ask.

"Spring mechanism."

"What's a spring mechanism?"

John doesn't answer, but he keeps taking the clock apart. A bolt here, a nut, then what looks like a circle of metal. He holds the circle like it's the circle at the center of the whole world. He's found the secret to everything.

"This is a spring mechanism," he says.

"What does it do?"

"When it's wound up it holds energy. Energy that's released gradually when..."

The spring suddenly springs with a big *BOING*, and now it's a much, much bigger circle all over the place. John is startled and calm at the same time. I think he doesn't want me to see him screw this up, so he acts like it was all planned.

"Yes, well, it just released its stored energy, see, that's what it does."

"Uh-huh."

John keeps taking the clock apart bit by bit. Pretty soon all the insides of the clock are laid out neatly on the newspaper. John looks at it for a long time. He's fascinated. It's all there, the spring, the little bolts, this piece, that piece. Amazing. Then he goes into the kitchen to get something to eat. I keep staring at all the pieces, waiting for John to come back. But he doesn't come back. For John, I guess, the interesting thing is taking things apart. That's when the secrets are

JOHN'S MACHINES

revealed. He's either not interested in putting the clock back together, or he can't, or both. Calvin could take apart a nuclear missile and put it back together so it works better than it did before—he may actually do that for a job someday. John's mind works different, that's all. He's really smart in his own way.

I go into the kitchen. John is two-thirds of the way through a box of Ritz Crackers. His cheeks are huge and his eyes look lost in clock-land.

"What do you want to do?" I ask him.

John shrugs. He doesn't know.

Payback

I'm so angry at John I just want to hit him, so I lunge. But he's much bigger and faster than me and darts out the door, laughing at my rage. I'm chasing him, my big feet in hand-me-down shoes clop, clopping over the driveway and lawn and onto the street. John is three steps ahead of me, laughing harder as he turns his head back to make sure I'm just a few paces behind—just far enough to make me feel frustrated that I can't quite catch up with him. We run down the street, around the block, up another street, a hill; I'm getting closer, then all of a sudden he just stops and turns around to face me. He isn't laughing any more. In fact, his mood has turned completely around to the somber, stone-faced look he often gets as he contemplates the world. He stands straight, at least 10 inches taller than me, and waits. I swing with my right fist and strike him hard on the side of his jaw. He flinches only slightly and keeps staring at me.

I feel this incredible release, and then emptiness. A blank. Why was I mad at him? I can't remember what he did that made me so damn mad. John will never hit me back. His stern, wounded silence is my punishment.

We walk home together.

Hiroshima Day

I'm finally old enough to climb Mount Washington in New Hampshire, the tallest mountain in New England. This is the annual climb that always takes place on the same day, August 6th—Hiroshima Day. It's the commemoration of the day the Americans dropped The Bomb on Hiroshima, and because Dad was on a ship in the Pacific then, and for a lot of other reasons, John, Nick, Calvin, Charley, Dad and me are making the climb. This is my first time. John, Nick, Charley and Calvin have been up I don't know how many times. And Dad, forget about it. He's been climbing his whole life.

It's sunny but not too muggy today, a good day to climb, Dad says. So we unload the packs from the back of the station wagon and check our stuff. I've got a big water bottle, a spare jacket (it can get really cold up there even in August) and a bag of what Dad calls

HIROSHIMA DAY

Grup. Grup is raisins and peanuts and whatever else Dad throws in that's crunchy. Energy food, he says. I take a handful bite from the bag and think it tastes pretty bad, sort of like something you'd feed a horse.

We start to climb. Nobody is saying much. We just climb and before long we're all breathing hard. Around the base of Tuckerman Ravine the trail runs through woods, past streams, and once in a while we'll get a glimpse of what might be the summit way, way up above us. My pack feels really heavy, but my legs are holding up OK. Farther on, the trees start to thin out. They can't take the hard wind, Dad tells me; the wind and the cold up here is some of the most severe on the planet. But within a few hours, a different type of wind has come to the mountain—right in front of me. Nick is farting up a storm.

"Stop farting!" I yell at him.

"That was John."

John laughs, "Nicky!"

"It was you!" I yell. The smell is incredible, and I can't believe it's still around. You'd think in a wind like this the smell wouldn't last, but Nick seems to hold the odor around him like a coat.

"Don't do it again!" I shout. Immediately Nick lets loose.

Dad laughs, "It's the Grup."

Now I see why I have to hold up the rear. Baby Teddy has to get all the Grup exhaust while the older brothers stay upwind.

When Nick isn't farting, I can enjoy the climb a bit more. The farther we go, the more we can see below us. The view is nice, with forest and fields way out toward the horizon. But over to the northwest, some clouds look like they're moving in. Dad says he's checked the forecast and we'll be OK. Not a storm to worry about.

We hike on. I'm covered with sweat. Nick keeps farting.

"Nick! Stop it!" I yell.

"That really wasn't me," Nick says.

"That was me," Calvin says. "I farted. What are you going to do about it, huh?"

What can I do? Nothing. I just hold my breath for a minute and hope for a gust of wind.

Within an hour we are enveloped in a cloud, and we're hiking over jagged, slippery wet rocks. The mist is so thick it doesn't have time to turn itself into rain. We are in the sky. All I can see is Nick, John, Charley, Calvin, Dad and the rocks about 15 feet beyond him on the steep mountain ahead of us. The rest is billowy white. I'm wondering how much longer this will take, when we'll be at the summit, finally, because I'm getting kind of tired from all this hiking and smelling horrible Grup farts, when through the mist above I see a pink Cadillac glide past. It's slow, whale-like, moving up at an angle and gone in seconds. The cloud opened for it, and closed behind it.

HIROSHIMA DAY

I'm sputtering, "Did you see that! Did you... was that..."

John laughs at me. "Didn't you know there was a road up Mount Washington?"

Nick says, "You've never seen a bumper sticker on a car that said, 'This car climbed Mt. Washington'?"

"No."

They all laugh at me and keep climbing. Very tired now, I feel that I'm hiking through some kind of dream. I keep expecting to see more cars glide past from any direction, Buicks, Chevys, Fords, fleets of cars floating on clouds. There's nothing, though, just mist. Until we get to the top.

I've climbed other mountains, smaller ones, and they sure as hell never looked like this place. It's like a hotel plunked down on the rocks. A snack bar is crowded. A fat woman holding a poodle shuffles by, and just past her is a Mt. Washington display showing how many hikers have died on the mountain due to severe weather. This is too weird; things don't match up. Poodles. Cadillacs. People who never climbed more than stairs. Deaths from overexposure. I snarf my Grup in wounded confusion. I swear when I go down I'm going to be in front and Nick and John are going to get it.

Dad buys us all a hot chocolate and it is by far the best hot chocolate I have ever tasted, and I tell everyone this more than once.

John asks, in between slurps, "Is it the best hot chocolate you've ever tasted or does it taste better now because you are wet and tired?"

"Does it matter?"

"Sure it matters."

"Why?"

Dad interrupts to explain the chemical interactions of the chocolate on our taste buds and the relationship to it all with our biology and little known scientific facts that blow clear over my head, except that I'm impressed that he seems to know what he's talking about and isn't it nice that I have a Dad who can not only climb mountains but also has a background in chemical engineering and went to MIT.

When Dad finishes, John says with his long expressive eyebrows and large brown eyes, "See? Told you."

After an hour or so on "the summit" we head out into the cloud for the descent. We start to hike down, but Dad stops us after a few minutes. He gets a small notepad out of his windbreaker and looks down at his notes. "I just want to say a few things," he says. The wind has risen and it's blowing his dark brown hair back away from his forehead. His eyes are squinting against the wind, and all around him, and behind, the shredded cloudy mist rushes past.

"Today is August 6th," Dad begins, "Hiroshima Day. On that morning, an atom bomb was dropped on

HIROSHIMA DAY

innocent Japanese civilians in the city of Hiroshima. Hundreds of thousands of people died instantly. Some were burned so fast, all that was left of them was a shadow on the ground. And hundreds of thousands more were left in terrible agony. Little children with third-degree burns." Dad pauses to switch note cards. I can't tell if he's crying. He might be. Or it could be the mist built up on his cheek. We wait a long time for Dad to continue. Finally he goes on, "When your mother and I were first married, before I joined the navy, we worked in a TNT factory. We helped to make the chemical that went into bombs. There was a large air intake vent in the TNT factory, and I used to scream into it, 'Die, you Nazi sons of bitches!' My hope was that the air in my lungs, and the intent of my words, would fuse with the TNT molecules and create a more powerful explosion. The TNT that your mother and I helped to make killed thousands of people, just like the Hiroshima blast. Whole cities in Germany were wiped out. Cities like Dresden with large civilian populations.

"When I was in the navy, at the Battle of Okinawa, my ship was dive-bombed by kamikazes. They were so close I could see their eyes—fanatical eyes. Men shouted—'Smoke, smoke!' and we made smoke to shroud the ship, making it harder for the Japanese to find us. Later, I saw pieces of the Japanese pilots floating in the water."

Dad changes note cards again. "My point is..." and

here he looks out toward a sky that's too cloudy to see and he stops talking for what seems like forever. Nick, John and I look at each other. Calvin and Charley are staring off into the clouds. We've all heard variations of this speech before, but Dad is being more emotional about it now. He's definitely crying; that can't all be mist. "My point is," Dad says finally, "all of us, you, me—we bear responsibility for their horrible deaths. Their terrible pain. It must never happen again. We have to gain a better understanding of human nature. We have to strive to reach the great goals of humanity. We must strive for world peace. And you, my sons, must be part of this great venture. That's it."

Dad tucks his notes back inside his windbreaker and starts down the mountain without another word. I'm still thinking about everything Dad said—it's pretty heavy after all—and before I know it all of my brothers and Dad have gotten ahead of me.

I'll be in back the whole way down.

What they don't know is that the wind is now in my favor. From here to the mountain's base I will inflict terrible pain on my brothers. They will strive to reach any breath of clean-smelling air. They will die horrible deaths. And I, Baby Teddy, will bear total, gleeful responsibility for their suffering.

Four Strong Winds

Calvin, sitting in our living room in Lexington, is playing his three records again. Ian & Sylvia, The Weavers, and Miriam Makeba. Mom and Dad have other records in the box, and Calvin gets records as gifts, but all he ever wants to play are these three.

Ian and Sylvia sing, *Four strong winds that blow lonely, seven seas that run high...*

Calvin is reading a *Popular Mechanics*. He won't talk to me if I say hi. He's just reading. There's a whole stack of *Popular Mechanics* magazines next to him.

But our good times are all gone, and I'm bound for moving on...

I'm having a bowl of ice cream in the dining room, watching, listening. Calvin turns a page; his eyes squint at some new story—probably an article about "Making Jet Engines at Home" or "Pipe Bombs on a Budget."

Four strong winds that blow lonely, seven seas that

run high...

I've heard this stupid song so many times it's driving me crazy. "Calvin," I ask him, "why don't you listen to other stuff?"

He doesn't answer. I try again. "Calvin? Um... I've heard this song about ten thousand times."

"So?"

"So... um... can you put on something else?"

"No."

"Why not?"

"Because everything else is crap, that's why."

But our good times are all gone, and I'm bound for moving on...

Nick comes downstairs; he's licking a Slim Jim and he's got another one in his pocket making a big grease stain on his shirt. He looks for a second at the record player like it's evil and he says to Calvin, "Jeez, Calvin, how about a little variety?"

Four strong winds that blow lonely, seven seas that run high...

Calvin sighs and turns the page. Nick looks disgusted and heads for the kitchen. Almost to himself, Calvin says, "Piglet."

Charley walks in from the kitchen on his way to his room. He says, "Hey Calvin, ever hear of the Beatles?"

"Why should I?"

Charley shakes his head and goes upstairs.

The song sounds very sad to me. The voices are

warm, Ian and Sylvia's together; it's a pretty song even if I have heard it a billion times. Sad and pretty. Calvin listens by himself. The pages turn. I wonder if he really did shoot the cats. I hope that—someday—he will be happy.

Then again, for Calvin, this may be his way of being happy. A stack of *Popular Mechanics* and a song that never changes.

But our good times are all gone, and I'm bound for moving on . . .

Dead Animals

Dad is in his "If we all work together we can find a cure for aging" phase, and he's developed the habit of bringing home dead animals. He finds a dead bird in the yard and puts it on top of the refrigerator.

Mom says, "What's that?"

"It's dead," Dad replies.

"You are off your rocker. Go bury the poor thing."

Mom pours milk onto my Corn Flakes. I stare at the bird. It's lying on its back, feet in the air, right on the corner of the Frigidaire. John is even less surprised by all of this than I am. He's cramming a loaf of bread into his mouth, a whole loaf, and his eyebrows rise up as if to say, *Well, isn't this amusing.*

Nobody moves the bird. It stays there, rotting slowly, its smell gradually spreading and filling up the whole kitchen.

Another day Dad brings home a dead duck he's

DEAD ANIMALS

found on the highway. Possibly to avoid nagging by my mother, Dad puts the duck in the big freezer in the basement. The duck is soon joined by a dead skunk.

I peer into the freezer to look at our animal morgue. The skunk, though frozen, still reeks. The wing of the duck is crusted with frost, nestled between cans of frozen orange juice. It occurs to me that what's probably brought all this about, all this thinking about aging and death, is my grandmother, his mother. Her name is Gaee (pronounced Ga-ee).

When I was little we used to go to her apartment in Boston. It was a dark place with a window that looked out on a brick wall, full of antiques and old photos in the living room of people I never knew. Even then Gaee seemed incredibly old to me. She was tall but bent, her hair dyed blue and curled, her eyes large behind her glasses. Her hands were always clasped around her chest and she smiled just about all the time. As soon as we arrived she dumped a jar of pennies on an old Persian rug. Little circles of copper on swirling dark blue and green. I could keep what I counted.

Gaee kept getting older and older. Muggers robbed her on the streets of Boston more than once. They held a hand over her eyes and took away her purse. And her health was going downhill all the time. Her eyes gradually lost their connection to her mind.

One day Dad and I visited Gaee in the nursing home. The nurses helped her into a wheelchair and we went out into the garden. The sun was amazingly white over everything, as if a camera flash stayed on, and even the red and pink roses paled in the glare. Dad pushed Gaee slowly over the brick path as I walked behind. Gaee's old age made me shy and awkward, and I hated the smell of urine—it was everywhere in the nursing home, even in the garden.

Dad stopped in front of a bush of roses. He carefully pinched off a flower that was well past its peak, all brown around the edges. He held it in front of Gaee's face. "Here Mom, see, this is a flower that has gone by." Gaee murmured something I couldn't hear. She held the flower.

Dad read every book he could get his hands on that related to the aging process. He founded a committee to study aging and what it all meant to society. And all the while the life in Gaee was fading out. Soon she was in a fetal position, unable to do anything by herself, her mind completely gone, her hair no longer dyed and curled; just straight and gray and short. Dad still came to see her as much as he could. He talked, told stories about growing up, did his best to jog her memory. Nothing worked. Everybody dies someday. Nothing lasts forever, although the smell of the frozen skunk has a pretty good shot.

I close the lid of the freezer.

Puppies

"Mom, when will Holly have the puppies?" I ask.

Mom is pouring macaroni into a pot the size of an oil tanker. John and I are hungry and she's not taking any chances. "Oh, the vet said any time now."

"Do you think she'll have them today?"

"Could be today. Could be tomorrow." She licks a ladle to clean it. "Listen, Teddy, there's no rushing Mother Nature. Holly will have the puppies when she's good and ready."

Holly waddles into the kitchen. It's hard to imagine her ever being a little puppy; she's so huge, a big brown bus of a dog. Her milk has come in already and her teats, like inverted teepees, hang down almost to the floor. "Holly!" I say. "You mother, you." I pet her broad flanks. Her tongue flops out and she pants. I say, "Aren't you a dog. Aren't you a good, incredibly fat dog."

"Oh don't say that," Mom says. "I know just how she feels. When I was pregnant with Nicky I thought I was going to explode. Your father barely got me to the hospital in time. That was a quick labor." Mom dumps a truckload of cheese into the pot. Holly maneuvers to her food dish and digs in.

"Calvin was the worst though. He was my first, so it's hard to say if I was just inexperienced, but it hurt plenty, believe me."

"What was I like?" I ask.

"You were easy. So was John. See," Mom stirs the pot, "when you have the first few you're kind of tight down there, you know? Then after that you loosen up. By the time you came along, whoooosh!"

I look over at Holly. She reminds me of an armadillo. I wonder if her puppies will go whoooosh. I can't wait to see this.

*

I'm lying in my bed reading a comic book in the room that is now mine but used to be Nick's before he left for college. The rocky Thing character from the *Fantastic Four* Marvel Comic is shouting, "It's clobber time!" and bashing the evil Doom through a brick wall. SOCK! KABOOM! KRRRRR-POW! I'm not sure who I like better, Thor or Thing. The whole Nordic superhero myth god theme is great, and Thor is the best of that bunch. His hammer is wicked; that's a word Chopper uses all the time and I find myself using it more and more. Thor is wicked cool. Thing is wicked awesome. The Human Flame is wicked, too. And those women with the really pointy breasts are the most wicked, even though me and Chopper don't talk about them. I sigh and put down the comic. The chalkboard in front of my bed still shows my life planned out by Dad: Period A, B, C, D, E.

Wicked.

I pick up another comic. *Spider-Man*. The most wicked thing about Spider-Man is his spider-sense. Any time something really bad is about to happen Spider-Man says (or thinks), "My spider-sense is tingling!" It really works, too. If I look at a real spider in my room from a distance it goes about its business. But if I walk up to maybe four feet away the spider freezes. I can tell his spider-sense is tingling. Whoever made up Spider-Man at Marvel Comics figured this out and that's what's wicked, that any grown-up could pay as much attention to spiders as a kid does. Spider-Man shoots out a web rope and swings through Manhattan. Somewhere in this canyon of buildings lies the evil...

There's a whimpering sound. I put down the comic. The sound stops. I pick up the comic. The whimpering starts again. It's a little sound. Could it be my stomach? No, my stomach doesn't make that noise. The sound keeps going, shuffle shuffle, whimper

whimper, sniffle. Where is it coming from? Nothing on the planet makes that noise, at least nothing that I keep in my room. Sniffle, snort. Oh jeez, it's coming from under my bed! I jump off the bed and look under and there's Holly and TWO PUPPIES!

"Mom!" I scream incredibly loudly right at Holly, who's looking guilty all of a sudden, "Mom, come quick, the puppies are under my bed! There's two now already, Mom! Mom, come now!" The big brown bus of Holly puts her tail between her legs and waddles away, leaving the two little passengers. What if something happens to the puppies under there? Where is Holly going with all those other puppy passengers? I can't deal with this...

"MOM!!!"

Mom walks in calmly, "It's all right, Teddy, this is all perfectly normal. She went under your bed to have the puppies because she wants to be comfortable, that's all." Mom reaches in to retrieve the puppies. I look around for Holly. She's gone.

Mom holds up the two puppies, one in each hand. They're éclairs. "Oh, aren't they cute?" Mom says. "Yes, and they're just fine. Just fine."

*

John and Mom corral Holly in one of the downstairs closets. Newspapers are spread on the floor, and one by

PUPPIES

one, puppies are popping out of Holly. John takes over as doctor. He kneels behind Holly and waits patiently. Holly strains, lifts her tail, and an éclair shoots out. Fresh from their mother's womb, the puppies are still in what Mom calls the placenta, a wobbly sack of goo. Holly eats it.

"Oh gross, John," I say, "don't let her eat it. That's sick."

"No, no," Mom says, "it's perfectly natural."

Sure, OK, but I'm still going to upchuck. Holly laps up the placenta and sometimes the puppy is moving and sometimes it's still. Dr. John looks at each one closely in the palm of his hand. If the puppy isn't moving he flings it up in the air as if he's making a pizza. "OK, puppy," he says, "time to be alive. Wake up and smell the coffee!" The puppy starts to wiggle around by the second or third fling.

A pile of puppies is growing on the floor. One. Two. Three. Four. Five. Six. Seven. Eight. Nine. Ten. Eleven. Twelve.

"Good girl," Mom says, petting Holly. "Twelve puppies. My goodness." Holly is lying on her side now. The puppies are scrambling for nipples. It's a fight because there aren't enough nipples to go around. That's life in a nutshell, I guess. Two puppies are left out; they crawl around whimpering; if they're lucky they push another puppy out of the way. Holly is exhausted. She's gone from big brown bus to milk truck in two hours.

Dr. John says authoritatively, "Now she'll sleep."

As I lie in my bed I can hear the puppies downstairs. The sound of 12 murmuring, milk-sucking puppies in unison is exactly the same as a large cocktail party.

*

Holly is having a terrible time with the nipple shortage. The puppies feed constantly. She can't sleep. Her teats look sore.

Mom bends down to stroke Holly's side. "Oh she'll be fine," Mom says. "Nobody ever said being a mother was easy. It never was for me, that's for sure. I breast-fed you guys plenty and I got sore; I know what it's like." Holly raises her head just a little. She's probably thinking, *Sure, but you never had 12 all at the same time.*

The puppies are beyond cute. When they're not feeding they crawl around with their eyes half open. They leave trails of poop on the newspaper. "Perfectly natural," Mom says, standing up.

But natural or not, Holly is definitely on nipple overload. Two puppies are missing the next morning; we look a long time for them and find them in the trash. Mom puts them back. That night two puppies are missing again. One is found in John's closet, the

PUPPIES

other under Mom's bed. We put them back. Holly, in her own wordless forlorn way, is crying desperately for our help and understanding—these are two puppies too many. Two puppies who didn't reserve their nipple tables in advance at the great mother dog bar.

Holly gets sick. Her teats dry up, and four of them are swollen and hard as rocks. We take her to the vet and he tells us Holly has developed an abscess. Sick breasts. She'll have to have surgery to remove the abscess. It's that or put her to sleep, an unthinkable option considering the brood of puppies at home. Holly will be in the pet hospital for a week.

A week. A whole week. And even when she's back, she won't be able to feed her 12 hungry puppies. I'm upset, but Mom is Mrs. Calm: "Don't you worry, kiddo, I know just what to do."

*

It's three o'clock in the morning and Mom and I are in the basement with the puppies. Newspapers are all over the floor, and boxes form a corral for the puppies.

Mom holds a puppy in her arms and gently offers a bottle. The puppy, its eyes closed, reaches for it with its little mouth. "You're hungry, aren't you? Yes you are."

Bottle-feeding 12 puppies is a major task—I can see what Holly was up against. The feedings are every three or four hours, 24 hours a day. We have boxes and boxes of formula and it seems like the puppies are always hungry. Mom, John and I are beat (John's asleep at the moment; it's not his shift).

I pick up a puppy and it starts sucking my finger. "Look at him, Mom!" We laugh together.

"I know," Mom says. "They're so little they don't know a nipple from a finger. It's instinct."

There's only one dim bulb above us in the dark basement. Shadowy benches, tools, the furnace and unknown shapes surround us. I give my puppy his bottle and he sucks happily. Puppies toddle around on the newspaper pooping and peeing and sniffing. It stinks and I couldn't care less.

Mom finishes feeding one puppy and picks up another. "Oh," she says, "I used to love to breast-feed. When Calvin and Charley were little, people just didn't breast-feed, you know; the doctors recommended the bottle. It wasn't until Nick came along that they started to say breast-feeding was better for the baby."

My puppy finishes his bottle. I set him down and pick up the one that's been pawing my leg. Mom continues, "Still, I think I only breast-fed Nick a little. John I breast-fed quite a lot, and you—oh you used to love to drink milk. I breast-fed you the most."

"Really?"

"Oh yes, hours and hours. To tell you the truth, and nobody talks about this, but breast-feeding feels terrific."

PUPPIES

"Yuck!"

"Don't be that way, Teddy, it's perfectly natural. And it's the best thing for you, they know that now."

I haven't had much sleep this week and I'm feeling kind of woozy. The edges of my vision are blurry. Another puppy is pawing at my leg, hungry, they're all hungry. They're like John.

"Sure, breast-feeding was a wonderful sensation," Mom says, picking up another puppy. "It was sexual, that's what it was. How else would Mother Nature get anyone to do it?"

"Mom, I don't want to talk about it."

"Why?"

"I just don't, that's all."

Mom laughs. "Teddy, don't be silly!"

"C'mon."

Mom chuckles. "You think it's dirty but it's not."

"I didn't say that."

Mom lifts up her shirt and unhooks her bra.

"Mom, what are you doing!"

"It's perfectly natural," she says, still chuckling. And before my eyes have had time to tell my brain what is going on, mom has the puppy at her big breast and it's sucking away.

"Mom!"

Mom's eyes roll up in her head. "Oooo!"

The puppy cocktail party has begun in earnest; mom is laughing hard, her whole body is rocking up and down—"Ooooo"—and the puppy is sucking and pawing at her breast with its tiny little claws. I can't be seeing this. Even if the best Playboy Playmate of the Year were breast-feeding a puppy it would be gross, and this is my mother—jeez, this is wicked strange. Mom can only take a few seconds of the puppy and then she puts it down. "Ooooh," Mom says, "I'm out of practice."

"Mom, you're a maniac."

"It takes a while to get toughened up."

A lot of the puppies are looking up at mom expectantly. Holly may be gone, but this new mom is here and all is right with the puppy universe. Mom looks down at the hungry puppies and sighs. "Goodness," she says. She hooks up her bra and pulls down her shirt. "Haven't done *that* in a while." She picks up another puppy and connects it to a bottle.

In our circle of light in the dark, poop-smelly basement at four a.m., a peaceful calm ensues. The puppies settle down one by one. They murmur among themselves. Some sleep. Mom cuddles her little furry brown baby in her arms—her last baby.

"Aren't you hungry? Yes, I know you are."

Death Molecule

I will live forever. And I'm with Chopper, who may live even longer. Chopper has just smoked a joint and he's very stoned.

Dad is in his 50s now, still in his "If we all work together we can find a cure for aging" phase. Today, as Chopper and I sit in the kitchen with the munchies, Dad rushes in and holds a large multi-colored molecular model three inches from Chopper's face.

"This," Dad says gravely, "is death." Then, without another word, he exits. Chopper's cheeks are stuffed with food, but he's stopped chewing. After this, Chopper doesn't come over much anymore.

Moving Boulders in the Brook

I'm lying on the beach reading a Hardy Boys book and Chet's in the middle of a speedboat race. The sun on my back feels great. I'm not quite hot enough to jump in the lake, but I'm getting there.

"Teddy!" It's Gramp. *Oh, shit*, I think, *he's found me.* I'm 12 and under his employ this summer to help take care of the family's rental cottages and land by the shores of Willoughby Lake. For 30 bucks a week I am a slave and there is no such thing as official time off. When I'm needed, I have to help. That's it. And there's no point trying to complain with Gramp. A biplane pilot in the First World War, he flew reconnaissance missions to photograph the enemy lines. In the Second World War, by then a full colonel, he helped Eisenhower prepare the Allies for the invasion of Normandy, checking supplies, stocking warehouses, and generally making sure all the i's were dotted and t's

MOVING BOULDERS IN THE BROOK

crossed. This is a man who knows how to get the job done. He's used to having his orders followed. Even now, bent with 70 years of living, Gramp's presence is commanding. He's tall, with a prominent nose and sharp eyes shaded by his long-brimmed khaki cap.

"Yes, Gramp?" I say.

"Teddy, there you are. I need your help in the brook." Gramp is leaning his weight against a thick steel crowbar longer than he is. I can't imagine what could be wrong with the brook, but all I can manage to say is, "Sure, Gramp." I put on an old pair of sneakers and follow him.

Cedar and birch trees lean over the banks of the brook and shade the clear water and the tumble of rocks. Some rocks are thick with a cushy green moss, some are polished by the current. I'm up to my ankles in the freezing water, still wondering what on earth Gramp is up to. He stands on the bank and hands the long heavy crowbar down to me. "Now Teddy," he says, "all we have to do is move that rock over to there."

"This one?" I ask, pointing the crowbar at a boulder that must be 400 pounds.

"Yes, move it over to there."

"Why?"

He doesn't answer. My grandfather must be getting senile; that's the only explanation. But senile or not, I better do as he says. So I try to lift up one edge of the boulder with my bare hands. It's like trying to budge a mountain.

"No, no," Gramp says testily, "use the bar. Get under it."

I do as he says. I use the bar as a lever, and with much gasping and grunting I move the rock about four inches.

"That's it, you're getting it. Keep at it, Teddy, keep at it."

I grunt more, I push, I heave. Sweat covers every inch of my body except my ankles, which are soaking in ice water. After a half hour or so I manage to shimmy the boulder over to the side of the bank. Finally, I can get back to my book, or maybe take a swim.

"That's just dandy," Gramp says. "Wonderful. Just dandy. We're almost done. Now all we have to do is move that rock there, yes—no, that one right there—yes, we have to move that rock over to there."

The rock he's pointing at looks like something out of Stonehenge. I stare at it for a second, imagining Druids performing ceremonies at its base. My protest is breathy and worthless. "That's an awfully big rock, Gramp."

"You can do it," Gramp says. "Just move it over to there and we'll be almost done."

It's always this way with Gramp, I realize—no matter where you are with a job, even if you've just started, you're almost done. It's a mental trick you can pull on yourself. But I am not done. I have to move this boulder, and that one, and that one, and that one, and

MOVING BOULDERS IN THE BROOK

this one, and that one, and my hands are soggy and raw from hauling at the rough, wet rocks; my toes are banged up and spongy; I'm an exhausted, sweaty, mindless mess, and all I have to do is move this other rock over to there, and that will be just dandy and we'll be almost done.

At long last, after seven hours in the brook, Gramp looks me in the eye and says, "Teddy, there's no substitute for hard work." I smile and look down into the shady water. The current is swift and straight right through the center of the brook. And the banks are lined with sturdy boulders that will prevent erosion of the valuable land. Next year the spring floods will do no harm.

Gramp adjusts his cap and walks off with the crowbar. "Just dandy," he says. "Wonderful. We're all done."

Nixon

Mom, Dad, me and John are sitting in front of the TV. The lights are off and we're painted bright gray by the TV screen. Nixon is giving a speech.

"You're nothing but a bucket of shit!" Mom yells at Nixon.

"C'mon, Janet, watch your language," Dad says.

"Just a big fat bucket of shit!"

This is the first time I've ever heard my mom swear, and she's really surprising me. Her face is lined deep with fury, her teeth are clenched. Nixon's talking about Watergate, and about how he's not a crook.

"You're lying!" Mom shouts, standing up.

I say, "He can't hear you."

"You're just a big fat steaming bucket of shit!"

Sapling Maples

Nick and I have been climbing up Mount Pisgah all morning. It's a hot August day. On lookouts along the way we've seen Willoughby Lake below us, blue and shimmering, with narrow white caps pushed along by the south wind. Now we're at the summit. No view. We touch the small bronze marker that means, "We did go all the way to the top," then we start running down the mountain.

It's a rush. We try to outdo each other, see who can go faster. I'm sucking air into my lungs and feeling the heavy thump of my feet, trying to think fast—which rock below will hold my weight, which stump won't be slippery—while around us the grove of young maple trees lets in only splashes of light that make the heavy undergrowth of ferns glow white-yellow. Now I'm going so fast I have to slow down, so I grab a slim maple with both hands and swing around, and the tree bends with me—it seems to bend forever—and I'm whipped around in a slowly slowing circle. The tree rights itself, and then I'm off again. I see Nick doing the same ahead, the tree arcing down, then he's running, and there is no other sound but our breathing and the thump of feet, and laughing, all the way to the bottom.

Fourth of July

"What are you going to wear?" I ask John.

"I think I'm going to be an ogre. There's got to be something here an ogre would wear." We're up at the summerhouse and John is digging through Mom's costume trunk, the one she found in the attic in Lexington. The trunk used to belong to some great aunt and uncle who died, Mom said. Of course, for them, these weren't costumes—they wore this stuff all the time. Clothes from the 1920s. Dresses and jackets and pants and muffs, long ropes of pink ostrich feathers. My costume this year is a swallowtail tuxedo. It's way too big for me but that's OK.

"John, I don't think they wore ogre clothes then."

John is determined. He keeps digging away. "Yeah, I know. But maybe something was added in later."

"I doubt it."

Mom calls up from downstairs. "Come on, boys,

they'll be starting soon!"

"John, there is no ogre outfit in the trunk!" John gets so determined sometimes he drives me nuts. Finally he stops digging. "OK," he says, "I know what to wear."

"What?"

"It's a surprise. I'll meet you at the beach."

John runs off with a purpose. I yank in my belt to keep my wide black tuxedo pants from falling down and then run after him down the stairs. He's gone. Out the door. Mom is in the kitchen. She's wearing a big billowy green flapper dress, a ring of frill around her head and a long feather boa around her shoulders.

"What do you think?" she says.

"Great, Mom!"

"Shall we go?"

*

The beach is a zoo. Nick is covered in green paint and wearing a tire around his waist, kind of a combo Jolly Green Giant and Michelin Man outfit; my cousin Sarah is a lumberjack. Aunt Lois, my mom's younger sister, is in a flag costume, basically a large bag that happens to be a flag with holes for her arms, and she's blowing "The Stars and Stripes Forever" on her trumpet. Various guests from the rental cottages are dressed up, too; there's a G.I. Joe, a Cinderella, an ant, a

FOURTH OF JULY

kid who wants to look like a gorilla (he's got brown cotton balls stuck all over his head), and two little twin girls around four years old who are pixies of some kind; they have little silver see-through wings and antennas. Everyone is running around on the grass that leads down to the beach by Willoughby Lake. We're showing off our costumes, laughing, excited. Then I see Gram and Gramp walking down from the farmhouse.

Lois stops playing the trumpet when she sees them. "Oh, my! Will you look at this! He's wearing his World War I air force uniform! And Mom is a Girl Scout leader!" They walk down the grass arm in arm. Gramp is stuffed into the khaki uniform; the buttons are about to pop off, and his pants won't close completely—he's got them held together with string. Still, you can see how handsome he must have been in the war.

"All right now," Gramp says, "where's the party?"

Lois starts playing "America the Beautiful" on her trumpet, and Mom gets out her accordion and plays along. Mom is good at playing the right notes but she can't manage the concept of rhythm. It's all stop and go with her. But Lois just plows ahead and people are singing along.

Sarah stomps up to me and says gruffly, "Got any trees I can chop down?"

I say in a stuffy voice, "Sir, gentlemen do not cut down trees."

Gram and Gramp are waltzing. The pixies are

skipping in tandem. Sarah's older brothers, Ted and Jeff White, are standing on the sidelines with some of the rental guests and they probably think we're nuts. Nick holds his tire around himself and bounces repeatedly into anything he can find: a tree, lumberjacks, G.I. Joes. Dad is carrying around a row of vertical metal bars seven feet long, anchored in wood at either end; around his neck is a sign that reads, "I Am a Prisoner of My Genes."

It's about five thirty in the afternoon, still sunny; the air is warm; Gramp has Pepsi and Fresca in the cooler, and it's not too buggy. All is good with America.

I bow to the pixies before me. "Madams," I say, "allow me to..." but the pixies become rigid with terror. At me? Why would they be scared of me? Their little blue doll eyes are wide with horror. One of them points to a place in the distance behind me. I turn.

John is at the top of the sloping grass by the road, towering over the world. He's naked except for his underwear and he's covered, all of him, with dark green mud. His brown eyes shine wild from the fierce mud mask. His hair is caked and gross like he's climbed dead from some long forgotten bog.

John bellows, his arms outstretched, "I AM MUD MAN!"

Lois stops playing the trumpet. Mom holds an accordion note until it wheezes out. There's a moment of silence, as if everyone is inhaling, and then the pixies

FOURTH OF JULY

scream and run for their mother. But their mother is not close by so they keep running in tight little pixie circles. Other little children drop their costume props and head for the woods. I'm thinking, *John, you maniac.*

Nick goes right along with the act. He bends down on one knee and does a Roman all-hail maneuver. "Yes! It is Mud Man!" John is so into the moment he has no idea he's scaring the little kids. Down from the road he marches, his big feet thumping the earth. "MUD MAN HAS COME!" he screams. John's broad white teeth are clenched in a vicious smile that shows through the mud.

Gramp says, "Well, isn't that something!"

Lumberjack Sarah says, "He must have rolled in the clay pits, I bet."

"MUD MAN REIGNS SUPREME!"

The pixies are like bugs around a lamp. Some of the rental guests are looking at each other, probably wondering what sort of mess they've gotten themselves into.

Mom says, "OK, everybody, get into line! It's time for the parade!"

All the kids in costume who haven't been scared into the woods by Mud Man line up behind Gramp. He holds an American flag. "OK, children," he says, "forward march!" Lois starts blaring "When the Saints Go Marching In" and we all sing along as we march. The pixies, reassured by their parents that John is not a real mud man but one of the Page boys (in reality, only a little less frightening), have calmed down enough to join the parade. My flapper mom pounds the ground with one foot, trying in vain to keep the rhythm. The saints go marching in anyway, all around the wide lawn. I dance in my tails. I wave my top hat at the crowds. Sarah giggles and raises her cardboard ax to the blue dusky sky.

Oh when the saints, go marchin' in, oh when the saints go marchin' in, Oh Lord I want to be in that number, when the saints go marchin' in . . .

"Wonderful!" Gramp shouts above the tumult. "Isn't this just wonderful! Oh yes."

*

The sun is starting to go down so Aunt Lois gets out the old newspapers. She holds court at the picnic table on the beach, a pile of newspapers on one side of her, the finished product—paper boats—on the other. Me and Sarah and a bunch of other kids are gathered around her. I guess I should figure out how she makes the boats, but she's so good at it I just let her do it. She's the boat lady and always has been. The boats are about a foot-and-a-half long, sort of like paper hats, but with crumpled balls of newspaper stuffed along each side. I hand two boats to the pixies. Sarah gets her boat. John and Nick and all the other kids have theirs too.

FOURTH OF JULY

Aunt Lois goes out on the dock and checks the conditions. A quarter penny of red sun is falling fast beneath the pine trees, and the color is spread out over the sky. The line of familiar mountains, Wheeler Mountain, Mount Hor, Mount Pisgah, and all the ridges in-between are reflecting themselves in the lake. There is no wind. Aunt Lois stands watching the last of the sun disappear, her hands supporting her back. "See how smooth it is?" Lois says. "Just like glass." And it's true. The whole lake, all five miles long and one mile wide of it, is flat glass. "OK," she says, "let's do the boats."

There's a rush of kids to the dock, all of us holding our boats and jostling for a good spot. Sarah and I are together. She leans over the edge of the dock and places her boat on the water. She puts a match to one of the crumpled-up pieces of newspaper. "Bon voyage," she says. I light my boat the same way. But I've also stuck extra matches into the sides of my boat, hidden in the newspaper, so they'll erupt in flames when the boat is way out on the lake. It's going to be great.

Soon a dozen boats are floating in flames.

"Look at mine!" the gorilla yells.

"Mine's really burning," the lumberjack says.

Nick's boat is huge; he's taped two or three together to make some kind of barge and it's a major flaming mass. "Burn, baby, burn," he says. Suddenly Mud Man's boat explodes in little firecracker bursts.

"Sabotage!" Mud Man yells. "The Nazi scum." The Human Flag starts playing "Auld Lang Syne." The boat fires are flickering, spread out here and there over the water, and each one is repeated in the mirror of the lake. Everyone is singing.

Should auld acquaintance be forgot...

One by one, the flames die. Blackened hulks sink into the sea. Drowning sailors shout for help, but this far out no one can hear them. My boat shows one last burst of flame—my hidden matches—then tips on its side and goes dark.

We'll take a cup of kindness yet, for auld lang syne.

*

My cousin Jeff lights a match to the bonfire by the edge of the lake, and within a minute the flames are huge. The heat is so intense that I can barely stand within 10 feet of it, even though I'm dripping wet from my swim. The bonfire, heaped with brush, logs and parts of an old bed, is as big as a burning house.

"Jeez," Sarah says, "that's hot." Sarah's blond wet hair is tangled down to either side of her face and she's bright orange in the fire's blare.

"I guess it is," I say. A spinning circle of light arcs out of the darkness farther down the beach—one of the kids is doing a sparkler. Now another one lights up. And another. They're trying to see who can spell their

FOURTH OF JULY

name before their sparkler goes out. I know that game.

Aunt Lois, Uncle Ray, Gram and Gramp, Mom and Dad, cousins and brothers are sitting on benches around the bonfire. Pixies are trying to roast marshmallows but their sticks aren't long enough—if they get to within roasting range, their wings start to smoke. Lois sings "God Bless America" and everyone joins along. I stare into the fire as my mind goes places where it's silent. I follow a spire of flame as it rises up, up into the air. This bonfire is so big it seems to go on and on, higher and higher. The flame reaches up as far as it can go and then it becomes a flurry of brilliant yellow sparks, and the sparks keep right on going. There are a lot of stars tonight. Sometimes it's hard to tell where the sparks end and the stars begin.

God bless America, my home sweet home. God bless America, my home sweet home.

Digging the Hobby Hole

"**N**o," pleads Nick. "Don't tell me! Don't!"

Mom inches toward him, a mischievous look on her face. Nick backs away. Mom says, "I just want to tell you the ending."

"DON'T TELL ME THE ENDING!"

"C'mon, it won't ruin it for you."

"Don't tell me ANYTHING!" Nick looks really desperate. His chubby face is contorted with anger and his red hair is a mess.

Then Mom delivers the lethal blow—"Frodo dies!"

Nick flips. He grabs a kitchen chair and flings it across the room where it crashes into the wall. One leg sticks into a new wall-hole so the chair stays there like some kind of museum installation.

"AAAAAHHHHH!" Nick screams.

"Mom," I say, "why did you tell Nick that?"

"He dies," Mom repeats. It's as if she's twisting the

blade in a dying man's chest. "Frodo dies."

Before storming out, Nick puts one more hole in the wall, this one with his fist. He's pretty strong these days.

Mom chuckles as she fixes herself another cup of coffee. "Well, I don't know what he's so upset about."

What he's so upset about is that Mom has supposedly told him the ending to *The Lord of the Rings*, J. R. R. Tolkien's trilogy. Nick is reading it for the first time, only halfway through the second book, and he really hates to have the story ruined. Mom understands this thoroughly, I think; she just enjoys getting a rise out of Nick. He rises much better than most people. And the new holes in the wall can be easily patched. The last hole he made was with his head—I can't even remember what he was mad about. It was a head-size hole, long since patched up.

I can understand why Nick is mad. It's amazing how any writer could create such a convincing fantasy world, down to the littlest details. Tolkien is brilliant. There are Orcs, monstrous nasty hairy beasts who are in the service of the ultimate evil power—Sauron. There are Elves, beautiful folk with Spock-like ears and magical stones and cloaks. There are Dwarves, long-bearded mineral miners who go to war with axes, Wizards such as Gandalf, Long Riders like Aragorn, and, of course, there are Hobbits.

Hobbits are short people with furry feet who prefer

to stay home, read a good book and drink tea. But one of their more interesting characteristics is that they live underground in Hobbit-holes. Entire villages live this way, and quite cozily. Not to be confused with nasty dirty holes in the ground, a Hobbit-hole is more like an English cottage that just happens to be under a hill. They are very clean and dry, no worms in sight. They often have windows that look out onto gardens. The better Hobbit-holes have many rooms. They go on seemingly forever into the hills, room after room, usually filled with cakes and other yummy food.

It is in this world that I am living at the age of 13. As Nick was, I am now in the middle of the second book of Tolkien's trilogy, and I'm two steps beyond enthralled. Aragorn is just about to . . .

"Ted."

It's my father, standing stern by my bunk bed in the summerhouse.

"Yes, Dad?"

"How would you like to build a Hobbit-hole?"

I'm thinking Dad is being philosophical. "That would be nice," I reply.

He says seriously, "There's a nice place for one up in the field. I've got the plans all ready. But I'll need your help."

"You really mean it? You want to build a Hobbit-hole?"

"Yes."

DIGGING THE HOBBY HOLE

This is the most exciting thing I've heard in a long time. Wow. A real Hobbit-hole, just like in the book. It's actually believable, too, because Dad designed our solar-heated summerhouse and built that. He should be able to pull it off.

I agree instantly to his suggestion. John is also pulled into the scheme. He's older than I am, but not so old that he can say no to our father, or that he's jaded like Charley and Calvin. And Nick is off at summer camp working as a counselor.

It all starts up in the field beyond the summerhouse. There's a rounded mound there that slopes down on one side, so it's easy for me to picture it as a Hobbit-hole. A window here, a cobblestone walkway there. We can build tunnels all through the field! It will be amazing!

Construction begins almost immediately. First, a backhoe scoops out a large circle, about 40 feet across. It's as if the mound has been flattened and deepened. Inside the lip of the hole the earth is then rounded into a dome shape. On top of this dome, Dad and several construction helpers intertwine steel rods which are laced together with wire. Then comes the cement truck, which pours a three-foot layer on top of and through the steel rods.

But the roof of the Hobbit-hole is not complete without a layer of meaning. Dad staples photos of burn victims from the Hiroshima blast onto six-foot-long foam core boards. He also adds pictures taken by inner city black kids that expressed their feelings about Martin Luther King, Jr.—a project Dad worked on with Polaroid. Dad lays the foam core boards down, photos facing the earth beneath, on top of the steel-reinforced concrete. The idea, Dad explains, is that the photos would radiate meaning into the concrete, fusing with the molecules, and create a kind of peace dome. Everyone living in the Hobbit-hole would feel the urgent need to bring about world peace. The backhoe shovels dirt over the whole thing and levels off the ground, so you'd never know there was anything under there.

The cement truck leaves. The construction guys leave. John and I stare down at the dirt. It doesn't look like a Hobbit-hole, I must admit, but you have to have faith in your father. Never show a fool unfinished work, and I'm no fool. Dad gives us a big hug and laughs. "A real Hobbit-hole," he says. "Won't this be something!"

"Now what do we do?" John asks.

Dad says, "We dig."

I'm a little incredulous. A large backhoe just left, and the three of us have been charged with going around to the side of the mound and digging under the four-foot steel-reinforced cement dome—by hand.

"That's going to take a long time," John says.

Dad wipes sweat from his brow with his handkerchief. "Well, yes."

DIGGING THE HOBBY HOLE

John states the obvious, because that's his job as the older brother. "Dad, why didn't we have the backhoe dig the whole thing out so we could build the walls and then put a roof over the walls and *then* cover it with dirt?"

"It wouldn't be a real Hobbit-hole then, would it," Dad states. I'm not sure what this means, and clearly neither does John, but when Dad tells us to do something there isn't much choice. We grab shovels and start to dig into the side of the mound.

Our tools include: shovels, picks, a wheelbarrow.

We start in July, just as the Vermont sun is getting hot. Work begins around eight a.m. Despite any misgivings I might have about the architecture, I'm still excited about the prospect of digging out a real Hobbit-hole. None of my friends will have one. In fact, nobody on the planet will have one. Lots of people get sucked into the fantasy world of *The Lord of the Rings*—what they call escapism. But for me this is escapism in reverse. I'm escaping into the real world of the Hobbit-hole. And these are the thoughts that fill my mind as I dig shovel after shovel into the red wheelbarrow.

A bumper sticker on the back of the wheelbarrow reads, "Dump war now. Dump Nixon in '72."

When the wheelbarrow is full, it takes all our strength to push it up the incline toward the dump-off point at the edge of the woods. We howl with the effort like samurai. After two weeks, we have dug to the outside edge of the concrete roof. Like archeologists, we jump up and down with excitement. We've created our own artifact, sure, but it's still a discovery.

Gramp stops by now and then to inspect our progress. "What do you call this thing?" he asks for the tenth time.

"It's a Hobbit-hole, Gramp," John says.

"A hobby hole?"

"No! A Hobbit-hole!" I say.

Gramp shakes his head. "Awful waste of time."

He stands there looking at us, his long face shaded by his broad khaki cap. Gramp has a practical streak that doesn't include the digging of Hobbit-holes. Finally, he shakes his head and walks off.

My cousins' father, Ray White, stops by occasionally, too. Ray walked across the length of Europe with the U.S. Army and swore never to walk again if he had some alternative mode of transportation. He's a man of gas-powered machines, the bigger the better. To him, the Hobbit-hole is the funniest damn thing he's ever seen. Proof positive that the man his wife's sister married is as crazy as he always knew he was. Dad scowls at him when he gets near.

"How's it comin', boys?" Ray says, grinning widely. He has big teeth.

"Great, Ray," John says.

Ray doesn't even bother to humor us with a compliment on our progress. He just chuckles.

DIGGING THE HOBBY HOLE

My mother is not very sympathetic, either. She won't go near the Hobbit-hole. And all she says to my dad about it is, "I'm going to bury you in that thing. It will be your mausoleum, how about that?"

I don't care. I'm a believer. I keep digging right alongside John and Dad. By the end of the first summer, we have dug a quarter of the way under the dome. It's now possible to stand inside what will be the Hobbit-hole. The roof is bumpy concrete, the walls, put up gradually as we dig inwards, are cinder blocks, the floor is dirt. Sure, it doesn't look like much now, but just wait and see.

"How's the hobby hole coming?" Gramp asks again.

"Great, Gramp, just great," I reply.

"Awful waste of time."

By the end of the second summer, now with Nick's help, we are two-thirds of the way through. Nick and I are taking full advantage of the subterranean acoustics. Like slaves, we swing the pickaxes to the beat of our spiritual songs. "Swing low, sweet chariot (wham), coming for to carry me home (wham)." The harmonies are beautiful, and the sweat that slips into my mouth adds its own flavor to the music. Over the course of this summer, and the last, my flabby teenage body has become hard. I'm starting to like this.

By the middle of the third summer, we have achieved the objective laid out for us by Dad. We have dug out all the dirt from under the dome, and put up the cinder block walls in a circle around the edge. This feels like a major achievement. It is our Great Wall. Our Egyptian pyramid. Our eighth Wonder of the World, right smack dab in the middle of a field in the Northeast Kingdom of Vermont.

Still, as September approaches, I'm wondering when it will start to look like a real Hobbit-hole. The floor is not only just dirt, it's muddy in places. Mosquitoes breed there. Spiders nest in droves along the edge of the roof. It smells dank and dirty and, most ominously, cracks have already begun to appear in the roof.

"I'm going to bury you in that damn thing," Mom tells Dad again. I wonder. Maybe she will after all, and me, too, and John and Nick. Just how stable is this thing? Dad assures us, along with all the doubters, that steel-reinforced concrete is not going to break under any circumstances. To prove how comfortable Dad is with the construction, he puts a desk in the middle of the Hobbit-hole and even has electric wiring put in. To keep the desk from sinking in the mud, he rests the legs on boards. One lone light bulb hangs down over the desk. Condensation builds up on the bulb, though, and if you try to turn it on by the pull cord you get a powerful electric shock. Dad writes letters at the desk. He reads. But he doesn't do anything to make the Hole really livable.

The next summer comes, and more cracks appear in the ceiling. Dad has moved on to other projects though, and the Hobbit-hole is put on the back burner. Charley and Calvin say it's a nuclear bomb shelter. Calvin says with a knowing leer, "Hobbits really don't need roofs with four feet of steel-reinforced concrete, do they?" When I ask Dad about this he just sips his tea.

All I can think about when I look into the Hole are the faces of the Hiroshima burn victims, staring down. They were in such pain, but their eyes were open a little, like they were asking that question Dad stuck to all our bathroom mirrors, the one he told us to never, ever stop asking.

Why!

Bella

I'm sitting at the kitchen table, getting ready to eat the chicken and mashed potatoes and carrots that Mom has cooked. Muttering to herself, she's hunched over the sink, rinsing a dish. It's 6:45 p.m. Dad is late.

"I don't know where the hell your father is," she says, "so you might as well start eating." I do as she says, and the chicken is pretty good, but Mom keeps muttering. She's pissed. "Your father's never around anyway, so what's the point? He comes home, he eats, he goes off to a meeting. He's always trying to save the world! Well, who gives a shit?"

I say, "He is doing some good things."

"He just makes me so damn mad I could scream," she says.

I know where this anger comes from. It's been building for a while, ever since a powerful new force appeared in Mom's life. It's ugly, fat and unstoppable,

BELLA

and its name is Bella Abzug. Bella is a politician from New York, a big strong woman with a large nose and a huge floppy hat. Bella isn't about to take crap from anybody. She says what's on her mind. And she has a lot on her mind. Mostly she talks about feminism. Why are women the ones who always have to cook? Why aren't women in positions of power? Is a man superior just because he has a penis? Huh? Who the hell put men in charge, anyway? To Mom, these questions are gasoline on the fire of her imprisoned soul.

Mom has taken to wearing big floppy-brimmed hats. She's joined NOW, the National Organization for Women. She's campaigning for equal rights. She attends meetings with LESBIANS—yes, they really are lesbians. She knows they're lesbians because one of them had a button pinned to her big floppy hat that said, "Like hell I'm straight." She's confused the name of Bilbo Baggins from *The Lord of the Rings* with a certain sex toy, and claims all the lesbians are using "dilbos" on each other. She goes to protests with friends.

And yet...

And yet...

... The traditions that Mom grew up with and have held her through most of her life still control her inner workings. Her brain has been hot-wired to serve men. Her husband. Her five growing sons. While feminism rages, Mom still cooks and cleans. She does everything she used to do. But now, thanks to Bella, she resents it more than ever. She seethes with remorse for her lot in life. She feels that she's missed her chance to do something worthwhile—because raising me and John and Nick and Charley and Calvin was not worthwhile, not really, that's just the jail cell society put her in. "I could have been an artist," she'd say wistfully. "I could have done anything." The traditions are too strong, though, for her to break away. All she can do is protest in her own way, at home. She can lash out at my father, the number one penis, the MAN who PUT HIS THING IN HER and made her have five babies that she had to feed and clothe and bathe and WHO PUT HIM IN CHARGE ANYWAY!

Dad walks in, places his briefcase by the door and runs into the bathroom. Mom leans against the sink and I can see the loathing radiate from her face as she listens to my father pee endlessly... with his penis. Dad comes out and sits at the table. Mom is still staring at him. Dad is dressed in a brand-new charcoal gray suit, with a thin tie dotted in a conservative pattern. Mom purses her lips. Then she turns back to the sink. And suddenly she spins around with a bowl full of soapy, oily water and splashes it all down my father's neck. He sits perfectly still, in shock, as the gray water drips down both sides of his suit.

Mom pauses for effect and then states, "How do you like that, you big dumb oaf?"

BELLA

I just stare at my mother and father. I don't know what's going to happen but I do know it's not going to be pretty. Dad is scowling, dripping, speechless. Mom starts to chuckle. "How do you like that?"

"Janet!" my father explodes. He hardly moves. His face is creased deep with anger.

Mom is still chuckling. She loves this. "All over your new suit. How do you like that?"

"Why did you *do* that?" Dad says through clenched teeth. "I have a meeting to go to."

Mom just laughs. To her, seeing my father thoroughly confused is a hoot. *But isn't it all obvious, Dad*, I'm thinking, *don't you see?* It's decades of servitude bundled into a bowl of greasy water. It's catharsis. Mom can't burn her bra—she needs it too much. This water, this one bowl, is all she can do. At this one moment in time, this is the most concentrated water on the planet. It's heavy water. It's holy water. And Dad has been forever baptized at the altar of the feminist movement.

The Great Meadow

"**G**ee, Skipper, can you really make a radio out of coconuts?"

"Why sure. If I can just get these spare radio parts that happened to wash up on shore to work I think we'll be in business, Gilligan!"

"Hooray! We'll be rescued!"

Dad shows up at the door of the TV room. It's actually a rectangle of Dad because he doesn't open the door all the way. I can tell he wants my attention but I sure wish he could wait until the end of the show. He just keeps standing there, looking at me. Mary Ann bounces in and talks to the Professor and I can't concentrate on what they're saying.

Dad opens the door a little wider. "Ted."

"Yes, Dad?"

"I thought perhaps we could go to the Great Meadow to look at microscopic life forms."

THE GREAT MEADOW

Mary Ann is almost bursting out of her bikini. "You're a genius, Professor!"

Oh no, I think, *not another nature hike*. I can't say no, though. Dad would get mad at me. "Sure, Dad!"

The Professor says, "Oh, not at all, Mary Ann. It's just basic science."

"You're too modest, Professor."

I turn off the TV, reluctantly, and follow Dad. He's dressed in khakis and a blue denim shirt and he's carrying the case. I'll miss the end of the show. Damn. But it's a sure bet they don't get off the island. It'll be on again, anyway.

Dad and I drive through downtown Lexington, past Woolworths and Doodlesacks drugstore, and down into East Lexington, home of the Great Meadow. We park behind the Unitarian church and Dad grabs the pack out of the back seat of the red Dodge Valiant. It's a late August afternoon and school will be starting soon. God, I hate school. The air is just cool enough to suggest that fall is coming; the trees are still green, though. Except for some of the really old maples along the path toward the meadow. Way up top some of the branches are showing bright red and yellow before they taper off to bare sticks. Dad's big hiking boots make scrunching noises in the gravel. We walk along without saying anything. I wish it were June again. Then the whole summer would be coming—I'd be headed up to Willoughby Lake to swim and sail and help Gramp with the cottages. But that will have to wait until next year. I'll just have to deal with ninth grade and get it over with. God I hate school.

The trees end abruptly just after we cross the railroad tracks and the meadow is before us. Tall grass and cattails straight out for miles, rolling up to small rock-covered hills, then down to broad flat areas. And it smells just like a swamp because that's mostly what it is. They should call it the Great Swamp.

"Ohhhh kaaaaay," Dad says. "Now, let's see what we can find." He walks ahead faster now, on a hunt. A window opens up in the cattails; he trudges through it and I follow right along. He stops here and there to look at something on a plant, then keeps going. Bugs buzz around my head and I'm getting bitten by something but I can't see what it is, which drives me crazy.

"OK, Ted, now I think..." His sentence trails off as we go up a rise. Five minutes later we've climbed up above the cattails and grass and we're on a small hill in the middle of the Great Meadow. I can see houses off in the distance just above a row of trees.

"... there's something here I wanted to look at. This lichen," Dad says. He takes the dark wood case out of his pack and lays it down on the ground very carefully. He opens the brass latches. His fingers move slowly, with anticipation; the lid is pulled back, and there it is: Dad's prized antique microscope. Its perfectly rounded cylinders are polished and smooth, gleaming gold in the late sun. He takes out the microscope and sets it on a smooth, flat rock on the ground. Then he picks up a small rock that's covered with lichen and flecks off a tiny piece of it. "Hand me a slide," Dad says. I give him one of the glass slides from the microscope case and he puts the lichen on it and sticks it under the lens. After a few adjustments he says, "Look at that. Amazing. Here, you take a look."

Dad shimmies over and I lie down on the rock next to him and look through the eyepiece. The lichen looks a lot like lichen under a microscope. Everything that was small is large. It's dull green. "Isn't that amazing?" Dad says. "This lichen is one of the toughest life forms on earth. It can survive blazing hot sun. Months without water. Extreme sub-zero temperatures. And it keeps right on living. Here, look at this one." Dad slips another slide in. It looks like another piece of lichen. I look at it and stand up. Dad takes over at the eyepiece. "Wow," Dad says, still looking through the eyepiece. "Never lose your sense of wonder, Ted. It's something adults lose as they grow older. Children have a sense of wonder but they lose it. If you can hold on to it, that's the key."

I'd like to feel a sense of wonder like Dad says and I'm pissed at myself that I don't. I don't even want to be here at all. I want to watch TV. I've seen lichen before, on rocks, on mountains, under microscopes. This is not new stuff to me; we've done it in school, too, and I hate school. I look down at Dad spread out on the rock looking through the microscope and I remember, all of a sudden, that Dad never really had a dad of his own. He was seven years old when his father died of tuberculosis; he's told me the story many times. Dad would sit by his father's bed, watching him slowly die. Sometimes he'd rub his father's chest to make it all better. One day his father wasn't there anymore. That night his mother told him that his father had died, and Dad, from that day forward, blamed himself for not being there to rub his father's chest back to health. It was all his fault. Seven years old and it was all his fault. I wish I could take the stupid guilt off my father's back, tell him it was *not* his fault; how could it be? But I can't do that. I'm helpless, too. There's only one thing I can do, and that is to try to be the son he wants me to be. Not the shallow idiot who watches *Gilligan's Island* and *Star Trek* and gets terrible grades, but the budding young scientist—like my father—who would have walked the Great Meadow with *his* father if the man had only lived long enough.

"Look at this one," Dad says, inserting another slide. I get down on the ground and look in the eyepiece. "Just look at those colors," Dad says. "Isn't that amazing?"

"Wow," I say, with all the honesty and sincerity I can muster. "You're right, Dad. This one is amazing."

Stronger Together

"I've got penis envy." That's what Mom announces during Thanksgiving dinner. "I just imagine it hanging there, you know? Just hanging there." She's saying this to everyone at the table, but she's looking directly at Aunt Connie.

In the 1930s Aunt Connie was a physical education instructor in Belmont, Massachusetts, lithe and beautiful. After getting married, she gave up teaching and bought a black-haired toy poodle which she named Spooky. Spooky died after a while. Then she bought another poodle, identical to the late Spooky, and named it Spooky. That Spooky died around the same time as her husband, so she went out and bought another Spooky, again identical. It died. She bought another Spooky when her daughter, Nancy, moved in with her. And this is the very old Spooky, mostly hairless, that lies next to Aunt Connie's ankle as she struggles to respond to my mother's penis envy.

"Now, Janet," my father says while carving the turkey with an electric knife that buzzes loudly, "you don't really have penis envy."

"I do, I do," Mom says, again staring directly at Aunt Connie. "Haven't you ever wanted one hanging there?"

Some old people look old on the outside, but are young on the inside. This is not the case with Aunt Connie; she's old through and through—as if the many years reading fragments of books in *Reader's Digest* and stroking bald patches onto a series of Spookys has aged her spirit far more than facial lines, gray hair or constipation.

"Well, . . ." Aunt Connie struggles.

Meanwhile, Calvin has taken all the potato skins, especially the ones covered with dirt, and put them in a blender. They came out looking like a perfectly respectable dip, which he now places in the center of the dining table. "Yummy," Calvin says. Charley, Nick, John and I are in on the joke, but Charley is looking guilty.

"I think it's because I had five boys, you know?" Mom says. "I always wanted to have a girl, but I had five boys."

"That's understandable," my uncle Hans offers. A first-generation Swedish American, he knows just what to say most often, which is usually nothing.

STRONGER TOGETHER

My cousin Karen, Hans's daughter, dips a Wheat Thin into the skin/dirt dip and pops it into her mouth. I can hear the grit crunching against her teeth. "Mmmm," she says, "nutty."

Aunt Connie looks to the floor. "Is Spooky hungry?" she says in a high, squeaky voice. "I'll bet Spooky is hungry. Spooky-wooky-wooky-coo." Spooky is around 98 in dog years, and apparently in his second childhood. Although my plate is heaped with delicious turkey all I can think about is vomiting. "Spooky-wooky, yes, Spooky-wooky!" Aunt Connie slips the poodle a piece of turkey. The room is instantly filled with loud gurgling noises as Spooky attacks the turkey with his toothless jaws.

Dad strikes an oratorical pose at the head of the table. Connie slurps up a wad of dip. "I think it's time," Dad says, "that we paused for a moment to think about the meaning of Thanksgiving." For important speeches, Dad measures each word, slowly. He's like a record played at a lower speed. The gurgling noises from below the table are as loud as ever. Calvin is snickering openly. Nick looks respectfully sheepish. John is bemused. I just want to get this whole thing over with so I can go outside and scream. "Thanksgiving," Dad says, "is a time of togetherness. A time when we, as a family, gather from many states to give thanks. And that's more than just thanks for good food."

Mom interjects, "I just hate it when he puts it in me."

Dad shakes his head and scowls at mom. She shuts up but has the look of a loaded gun with the safety off. Dad takes out a single wooden dowel about two feet long and three-quarters of an inch thick. "This dowel represents a single person alone in the world." He puts the dowel against his knee and breaks it easily. "Alone, without our family, we are weak." Then he holds up seven dowels, all bound together with red, white and blue ribbon. An American theme, I'm guessing. He puts them against his knee and tries to break them. His face turns red, then a Maxfield Parrish blue, and just before his head seems about to explode he puts the unbroken dowels down on the table. "Together, as a family, we are strong."

There is a pause. All I can hear is Spooky gumming and snorting. I'm thinking that Dad is right about being strong together, I guess, but if that means hanging around with Aunt Connie and her poodle I'm not sure it's worth it.

When we're done with dinner, Dad unveils a new invention from Polaroid that he's very excited about. Instead of just a camera that takes instant pictures, this invention—which we are getting a sneak preview of— takes instant color silent movies. The camera looks a lot like the Super 8 camera we used to have, except that instant color motion picture film (Dad explains) requires a lot more light. So on top of the camera are two extremely bright lamps. Dad powers up the

STRONGER TOGETHER

"Polavision" camera and starts to film us, moving slowly from room to room. The only problem is that the lights are so incredibly bright, everyone is blinded and has to hold their hands up over their eyes. Instead of a relaxing post-Thanksgiving meal family time, it's like Dad is a prison guard shining a searchlight down on panicked escapees. When we pop the instant film cassette into the combo developer/viewer box, all of us huddled around to experience Polaroid's future unveiled in all its glory, we see the newly recaptured prisoners being interrogated under the harsh lights, our grainy Polacolor faces bleached white in the glare, arms raised up over our eyes as if to ward off a blow, Aunt Connie trying to smile politely, and me and my brothers laughing and running in all directions to avoid being filmed.

Band

"You look really great. Really great," says Mr. Gillespie. He's in the center of the football field talking into a megaphone. "All the fund drives really, really paid off. You have the best, sharpest uniforms I have ever seen. And I've been teaching for 40 years so I should know."

The cheerleaders squeal with happiness. "Yaaaaaay!"

"I feel like an idiot," Tom says, and then he empties the spit valve of his trombone. It's a cold September day and the high school band is getting ready to practice marching in formation.

"You *look* like an idiot, too," I tell Tom. I empty my trombone's valve.

"So do you."

He's right, of course. While most of the band uniform is what we expected, solid blue with gold trim—the school colors—each hat is topped with a

BAND

large clump of yellow feathers. It's kind of like having a dead parakeet perched on your head. A dead pom-pom bird.

"Just shoot me and put me out of my misery," Tom says.

Mr. Gillespie, about 60 years old, bald, with a quarter-sized pale mole to the right of his nose, yells, "OK, let's get into formation for 'The Stars and Stripes'!"

The cheerleaders in their short skirts and new breasts bounce up and down enthusiastically. The whole band, about 50 of us, start to scramble around on the field. At my height, six foot six, my view is mostly of the dead yellow pom-pom birds flying this way and that, a confused flock. The trombones, saxes, flutes, trumpets, tubas, clarinets, French horns and (of course) the lonely but cute xylophonist have no clue as to where they should be. Me included. I took notes when Mr. Gillespie told us but I can't read the scribbles on the margins of "The Stars and Stripes Forever" music attached to my trombone's lyre.

"No, no!" Mr. Gillespie shouts. "Clarinets over here. Over here! Jimmy, I told you! Didn't I tell... Mary! This way!"

The dead yellow pom-pom birds seem frightened. Some are frozen in one spot. Others move with false confidence in one direction only to change direction a moment later.

"Tommy! Ted! Where are you going?"

"Um."

"Right here! That's where I told you to be, isn't it?" Mr. Gillespie has the megaphone right in my face and it's deafening. "Right?"

"Um. Yes. OK."

After half an hour we're lined up in the right starting points. Then Mr. Gillespie raises one arm and says, "One, two, ready, GO!"

The march begins.

My lips are pursed against the cold mouthpiece and the sound that comes out of the trombone is like a pregnant cow. And all around me other hideous squealing noises have erupted. My feet are on autopilot, marching up and down just like Mr. Gillespie taught us. And my scribbled notes say that I need to go straight ahead for two measures, that's eight beats, then take a sharp RIGHT. I take the right but Tom, in front of me, turns LEFT. Through the mouthpiece, and in the middle of a pregnant cow moan, I try to call to Tom, but it's no use. And I have no idea if I'm going in the right direction or if he is. There is another trombonist, but she's behind me and I have to turn slightly to see if she's there—she is. Unfortunately, in the process of turning to see her I've gone a little off course and now I'm heading straight toward a tuba. The dead yellow pom-pom birds are going every which way now, the music is deafeningly bad, and Mr. Gillespie is bellowing

BAND

above the tumult, "No, no! What are you doing! Billy, turn left! LEFFFFFT!" I turn at the last moment to avoid the tuba. I look around for Tom. He's way off with the flutes. The other trombonist is still following me, even though I can't possibly be going the right way. I've long since given up on following any predesigned path, but I figure it's better to move confidently in the wrong direction than just stop. Besides, somebody's bound to hit me if I stop. The band, I dimly remember, is supposed to be creating a formation that looks like a star when seen from above. The fact that the school bleachers are not high enough for anyone to actually see the star has somehow been lost on Mr. Gillespie, unless he's counting on an accidental viewing by a plane. And in any case, our formation would more closely resemble the chaos of the universe, each of us individual stars moving aimlessly in a vast green grass galaxy.

Suddenly a cheerleader's baton spins out of the heavens and lands on my trombone slide. The dent is large.

Mr. Gillespie finally stops the carnage. He stands on a bleacher, megaphone at his side, his head slumped in aggravated grief. We've let him down. I take off my hat and stroke the feathers of my dead yellow pom-pom bird. I hear a giggle. It's Janet, the cute xylophone player. Our eyes meet. She's trying not to laugh and not doing a very good job of it. I wonder what she looks like naked.

She Who Makes All Things Grow

Mom stands like the Lord of All Green Things in her Vermont garden. Hands propped behind her back, she looks down regally at her pride and joy. Peas bursting from their pods. Long green beans thick on the vine. Lush tomatoes. Scallions. Onions. Potatoes. Corn shoulder-high in the August sun.

"I don't know how I'm going to can all this stuff," she sighs. "And I can't give it away."

"We'll just have to eat a lot, I guess," I tell her.

She snorts, "Look at these peas!" She bends down and picks a pod off a vine and bites into it. "Delicious." She walks down a row.

I'm in between chores for Gramp, my last full summer as the official slave of Willoughby Farm, my last year of high school coming up. Once in a while, when I have time, I help out Mom in her garden. Some people have a green thumb. Mom has a green presence.

SHE WHO MAKES ALL THINGS GROW

Simply being around her makes vegetables grow faster. She is a walking, breathing container of Miracle-Gro. I can practically see the vines sprouting faster in her path. Then she stops before a tall leafy plant at the end of the row.

"This is your plant," she says. "What did you say it was?"

"It's a pot plant. Marijuana." I wait for her reaction. She just chuckles and says, "You're going through a phase, Teddy, that's all. You're trying to rebel because you're a teenager."

This is the problem with being the last of five boys. She's already seen every phase I will go through four times already. How can I rebel when she knows exactly what to expect?

I try again. "It's for smoking," I say. "It gets you high."

Mom goes back to picking peas. "You'll grow out of it."

Dad knew about the pot plant a while ago and all he did was get a book out of the library called *Marijuana Revisited*. It was written by a Harvard researcher, and it basically said, according to Dad, that pot was relatively benign. Dad never even mentioned the pot plant to me again. Where is the justice in that?

Mom munches as many peas as she picks. "Your brother Calvin was into all sorts of things. He grew out of it. He's doing fine. Charley was a hippy, you know—

who knows what he did."

"Plenty, I'd guess."

"Oh, I'm sure. But look at him now."

This whole pot plant thing is a waste of time. I should be doing something more outrageous. Sex? Definitely.

It's getting hotter and hotter. Time for a swim. "I'll catch you later, Mom."

"We're having dinner at Lois's tonight. Around six o'clock."

"OK."

*

Aunt Lois, Gram, Mom, Dad and I are sitting at the picnic table on Lois's porch overlooking Willoughby Lake. Lois has made fresh corn on the cob from her garden, there's grilled chicken, and mom has brought coleslaw made with a cabbage out of our garden.

"Mmm," Mom says. "This corn is so sweet. Ambrosia."

"Ambrosia," Gram echoes. Though very old and frail, Gram still has her own teeth. She chews down the ear of corn like an ancient raccoon.

Lois downs some coleslaw and says, "And this cabbage is from your garden, Janet?"

"Huge cabbage this year," Mom replies. Now she, too, eats the coleslaw. Gram takes a bit, too. "This is awfully good, Janet."

"Oh," Lois says, "that's the best coleslaw I've had in ages. And what's this herb, Janet? Is it parsley?" I look in the bowl. The cabbage and mayonnaise is flecked with green.

Mom says, "Yes, parsley." She winks at me. What's going on?

Dad says, "History will not be kind to Nixon."

I mouth the word *WHAT?* to Mom. Her answer is a quick glance at the coleslaw. I still don't know what she's talking about. So she gets a forkful and picks out a piece of the green fleck without anyone noticing. She waves it a little, then puts it back on the fork and mouths the word *POT*.

Oh God. Oh no.

Gram interjects, "Say what you will, Bill, but I still think he was a fine president." She helps herself to more slaw. No, not the coleslaw. My mother is drugging my staunch Republican grandmother. This can't be happening. The whole table is snarfing it down. Oh God, no. I try to take the bowl away but Lois reaches for the spoon. "Hold on, Teddy, we're not done with this."

Any mention of Nixon in a positive light makes Mom apoplectic. She sputters, "He was a crook, that's what."

"No, Janet," Gram says patiently, a mother correcting her wayward daughter.

"Sure he was. He got caught with his shitty pants down."

Dad says, "Must you swear at the dinner table?"

I'm staring at the disappearing coleslaw and wondering if, uncooked, it will have any effect on my relatives. I ate it once in a brownie and got so stoned I had to stagger out of the movie theater. Granted it was *Andy Warhol's Frankenstein* and I might have staggered out even if I hadn't been high as a plane, but what on earth am I going to do if my 94-year-old grandmother ODs?

Lois yawns wide. "Goodness, I don't know why I'm so sleepy."

It's started.

Gram's eyes are lidded and feisty. She says, "Nixon was caught doing something every American president has done, that's all."

"He was a big bucket of shit," mom says.

"Janet!" My father says sharply.

Gram yawns, "I think I need a nap, that's my problem."

Lois can't keep her eyes open. And to make the situation even worse, she has a glass of wine. Mom doesn't seem to be affected by the slaw. Or maybe she just always acts a little stoned so I don't notice. Mom says, "Course he was. I'm not saying anything that isn't true."

Gram would love to keep arguing but she needs to

be horizontal. She reaches for her cane. "Lois, I'll just lie on your couch."

Mom winks at me and chuckles. She says to Gram, "Are you sure you wouldn't like more coleslaw?"

Gram shakes her head. "I'm all done."

"Well I guess you are!"

"Bill," Mom says, "you finish it up." She ladles it onto his plate and he keeps eating.

Lois yawns again. This yawn lasts forever; it's like she has lockjaw. Mom says, "Maybe you should have a nap, too, Lois."

Lois waves the suggestion away. "No, no, I'm fine. I have too much to do. I have to finish making that car for Millie's wedding. And I have to bring the dress in to the garage."

I put my head in my hands. Mom has done it again. No matter how much I've rebelled, it's just pissing in the wind of her ongoing hurricane of outrageousness. It's as if she's saying to me, "So you think you're rebelling? Look at this, buster!" I excuse myself from the table as Dad eats the rest of the slaw and Lois falls asleep in her chair.

Mom's eyes shine with mischief and delight. "See you, kiddo," she says.

"Behave yourself," I reply.

She chuckles, wipes her mouth with a napkin, and studies my unsuspecting father. Her fun has just begun.

The Pineapple

Me and my high school buddies—Jim Stetson, Charlie Ferranti, and Ian White—have a wicked case of the munchies. We creep into my kitchen, whispering, giggling. "I'm still seeing tracers," Charlie says.

"This must be really good acid," Ian says.

"Really good," Jim says.

They sit around the kitchen table expectantly. "What do you have to eat?" Charlie asks.

I open the food cupboard. There's a big can of flour. A smaller can of sugar. Lots of spices in little jars. A jug of molasses. Coffee. Coffee creamer. Bread crumbs. Baking soda. Baking powder. Brown sugar. Gravy Master. Cake frosting. Food coloring. And a large container of salt.

"Any Cheez Doodles?" Jim asks.

"Well," I tell them, "the problem is that my mom makes everything from scratch."

THE PINEAPPLE

Charlie looks crushed. "What are you telling us?"

I'm starting to giggle. "I'm saying, we can eat here, but we'll have to spend a few hours baking first."

Everybody laughs. "Oh man," Charlie says, "your mom is the greatest. I don't think my mom ever made anything from scratch."

"Hey, we have to be quiet!" I tell them. "I don't want Mom to wake up and..."

Mom walks into the kitchen. "Hi, boys." She's wearing a nightgown that juts out over her breasts then goes straight down to the floor. It's as if she's wearing a box like the tap-dancing cigarette packs in the old TV commercials.

"Hi, Mrs. Page," everybody says with forced normalcy.

The hungry LSD-warped baby birds are sitting around the table, their faces bright under the suspended lamp, staring up at my mom with shit-eating grins. My friends know my mom. They know what to expect, which is that they should expect anything and everything. They watch her with fear and wonder. An eccentric God-like Mother Earth woman who could disembowel them with a comment, or toss them into hysterics with a sly off-hand joke. We are at her mercy now. Anything she does could set us off and we'd all dissolve on the floor in hysterics, exposing the fact that we are on drugs.

"Whatcha doin'?" she asks, getting herself a glass of

water.

"Looking for a snack," I reply.

"There's not much in the house. Do you want some leftover chicken?"

She ignores me and pulls a chicken carcass out of the fridge. "Mom, I really don't want any chicken."

She holds the chicken in front of Charlie. "Don't you want some chicken, Charlie? It's good."

"No thank you, Mrs. Page."

Mom ponders Charlie for a moment. I wonder if she can sense anything. A smell, the wild look in his eyes, the way he's smiling for no particular reason.

"It's going to go to waste if you don't eat it up."

Jim and Ian are twiddling their thumbs, trying not to laugh. Mom makes a "tsk" sound. "Well, it's in the fridge if you want it."

"Mom," I say, "is there anything else to eat, like crackers or popcorn or something?"

Mom shakes her head for a second, then brightens. "Oh, eat this up." She takes something out of a bag that's been hidden behind the toaster and places it in the middle of the table, directly under the lamp.

It's a pineapple.

"I'm going back to bed," Mom says. "See you, boys."

"Good night, Mom."

"Good night, Mrs. Page."

We are left alone with the pineapple. It just sits there. There's a pause—not only a pause in conversation,

THE PINEAPPLE

but also in thought itself. The pineapple has stunned us. Finally, Charlie says, "I could go for a pineapple."

Jim says, "I like pineapple."

"Pineapple is good," Ian says.

Charlie laughs, "Let's cut the sucker up!"

I giggle and take out a long butcher knife and cutting board. As soon as I touch the pineapple, though, a strange realization strikes me. The pineapple is *alive*. Its fresh skin is green and yellow. Its fronds stick out like a boy's unkempt hair. And even beyond any imagined resemblance to a human, the fruit is alive, in a pineapply sort of way. And why not? It was taken from the tree not too long ago. If it was planted it would grow into a pineapple tree. It is alive.

"What's wrong?" Charlie asks.

"I . . . the pineapple . . . I . . ."

"Come on! Slice it up! I'm starving!"

He's right. This is ridiculous. I put the edge of the knife against the jaggy edge, but my resolve lasts only a second.

"I can't do it."

"What do you mean you can't do it?" Charlie says.

"It's murder."

This is too much for them. They erupt in laughter again, and I'm laughing, too, and I know it's stupid as hell but I just can't help it.

"Look at the poor thing! Can't you see? It's just as alive as we are!"

They stop and stare at the pineapple. Ten seconds pass. Then Charlie says, "Oh man, you're right. It is alive!"

"It is," Jim says.

"What are we going to do now?" Charlie says. "I'm hungry. Come on, we're on top of the food chain!"

"Then *you* cut it," I tell him.

Charlie takes the knife. He's just about to cut it, but puts down the knife. "I feel really bad about this."

"See?"

Ian takes out a cigarette and lays it on one of the pineapple's fronds. "We'll make it an execution, then," he says. I'm laughing so hard I can barely sit in my chair. Ian lights the cigarette. The smoke spirals up in a brilliant white string toward the light. The poor little pineapple is having its last smoke, and it knows it.

The Accidental Guardian

My father braced himself against the high wind, his hands shaking with age, his gray hair swept sideways. Rags of mist blew past like tumbleweed over the jagged rocks, and down below, about a quarter mile distant, the Lake of the Clouds came into view, then out, obscured by the fast-moving clouds. It could have been a scene from *Macbeth*, but we were actually on Mount Washington again—me, my father and my brother John.

For years, it had been a family tradition that we climb on Hiroshima Day, August 6th, to honor the victims of the blast. Throughout the 1970s we made it just about every year. Back then all five brothers made the trek, following Dad up the steep slopes of New England's highest mountain. By last year, though, John and I were the only ones willing and able to go.

Dad took out his notes. It was time for "the

speech." John and I had heard it a million times before, but somehow it still got to me. Dad spoke of the war in the Pacific. Kamikazes diving at his ship, so close he could see the fanatical eyes of the pilots, the American sailors shouting for smoke to screen the ships, the explosions, the horror. He said to himself, "Oh God, just let me live through this day and I will do good things for the world. Just let me live today, please God." He spoke of the atomic bomb. There was just no way, in his view, to justify the annihilation of a city. Everyone shared the guilt, he said.

There was a time I used to protest: "But Dad, you were at Okinawa. If Truman hadn't dropped the bomb, you probably would have died in the invasion of Japan."

Dad would shake his head sadly. "There's always a way to rationalize cruelty," he'd say.

This time, though, I just let him speak. I had the feeling this would be our final trip up the mountain.

Dad said it was our duty to carry on his work. The world needed to better understand human nature so that we could avoid war. John and I sat and listened without talking. The wind made a whistling sound through the crevices, and I could sense the ghosts of our past selves, all the brothers together, climbing over these same rocks.

John and I were just starting to get up, thinking the speech was over, when Dad said, "There's one last thing I need to tell you. It's a true story."

John and I looked at each other, wondering. We'd heard the speech many times before and this was not part of it.

"Something happened a long time ago," Dad said slowly, "that put things into perspective. I was waiting to board a flight in Los Angeles and this woman—she was a total stranger—came up to me and said: 'Excuse me. I was wondering if you could do me a favor. I understand you have a ticket for the earlier flight. Would you mind switching seats with me?' Well, she took my seat. And I took her seat on the later plane."

Dad paused for a moment. He looked me in the eye. Then he said, "Her plane crashed. Everyone on that plane died. And I would have died, too, if she hadn't taken my place. So, you see, this is all grace. All the years since then, grace. Every day I'm alive is a gift. And I can't waste that gift. It's too precious."

John and I were stunned. Finally, John said, "This happened?"

"Yes."

"When was this?" I asked.

"Oh," he replied, "years ago. Before you were born."

"So what you're saying is that if this woman hadn't switched seats with you, I would never have been born?"

My father nodded. "Yes, Ted, you would never have been born."

I was shocked. Dumbfounded. The whole thing felt

like something out of *It's a Wonderful Life*, the old Frank Capra movie. In the film, a guardian angel named Clarence jumps off a bridge to prevent George Bailey—the Jimmy Stewart character—from taking his own life. At the end of the film, when George hugs his daughter by the Christmas tree and she reminds him that every time a bell rings an angel gets his wings, forget it. I blubber like a big baby. All six feet six inches of me.

We resumed our hike, but in the days and months that followed I found myself preoccupied with questions. If William Page had died young—and I had never been born—what would the world be like? Exactly where and when did this crash take place? Who was this mystery guardian angel who saved my father's life?

I hunted for information. And what I found blew me away. My father had escaped the most horrific air disaster that had ever occurred in America up to that time. It was June 30, 1956. A TWA Super Constellation and a United Airlines DC-7 collided in midair, then crashed into the Grand Canyon. Everyone on both planes died—128 people. The first domestic crash ever for either type of plane. The first civilian midair collision over the United States—and in the wide-open spaces of the Great American West. Americans were used to thinking of the West as incredibly vast, and suddenly, in one split second, the frontier skies had limits. Hopi and

THE ACCIDENTAL GUARDIAN

Navajo Indians held a 24-hour prayer vigil for the dead.

The *New York Times* showed a list of the passengers of both planes. Who was this mysterious woman? I badgered Dad with questions. He remembered she was not from California, and she needed to get home to her family. She was mature. Anglo-Saxon. I scanned the list. For the first time in my life I had an inkling of how people feel when they're hunting for their biological mothers. After all, this woman, like my mom, was responsible for my existence.

I asked United Airlines for help in finding her, but they said I was looking for a needle in a haystack. It's just as well. What would I do if I found her? Hey, folks, don't feel so bad—your wife/mother/grandmother died, but look what I have as a result?

So I'll refer to the mystery woman as Kate. I picture her in the Los Angeles airport in 1956. She's probably medium height, 43 years old, wearing pearls. Her blue dress is classic '50s. She rushes into the crowded waiting area, where many people are trying to get on the nine a.m. UAL flight. The airline can't help her; the flight is booked. She scans the room for someone she can ask a favor of. And then, in the same way the flick of a butterfly's wing can set off a chain of events that lead to a hurricane, her eyelids flutter. Blink, blink. There's a balding man in a bow tie. No, not him. Blink. That other one there. Hmm. No, he looks cross. Blink. Blink...blink. That man...

Kate sees my father. He's tall, in a charcoal gray suit, white shirt, thin tie. He has Gregory Peck good looks, black-rimmed glasses, dark brown hair neatly combed. Him.

"Excuse me, sir, I was wondering if you could do me a favor."

Dad's a gentleman, always has been. He opens doors for people. Even in Cambridge's nasty rush-hour traffic, he lets people go ahead of him, never swearing, always cool and calm. No matter how much the world swirls around him, he finds a way to be the eye of the storm. So when he sees Kate before him in the hectic terminal, he agrees on the spot. They go to the counter and exchange tickets.

Kate boards the flight. Out of her window she can see another plane—a beautiful craft with three tails and four propellers. Very distinctive. Kate doesn't know it yet, but this other plane is a TWA Super Constellation. It will leave L.A. three minutes ahead of her.

Kate settles down to read her book. Perhaps it's *The Quiet American*, by Graham Greene, a *New York Times* Best Seller that week. She thinks, *Thank goodness that nice man let me use his ticket.*

Kate reads quietly, then falls asleep. About an hour later, the voice of Captain Robert F. Shirley wakes her. "Ladies and gentlemen, we're just passing over the Grand Canyon. There are some pretty big thunderheads 'round these parts today, but I think I'll be able to steer clear of them to give you a better look." Kate stares out her window. Her jaw drops in wonder. Majestic towers of rock, and two rivers running deep through the rock. "The larger river is the Colorado," the captain explains, "and the smaller river—the blue one—is the Little Colorado."

Turquoise, Kate thinks, *like an Indian necklace. How pretty.*

At 10:31 a.m. and 21,000 feet, there's a sudden fierce jolt as the TWA Super Constellation and the United DC-7 collide. The tail of the Constellation is torn off, its fuselage ripped open from the tail to near the main cabin door; the DC-7's left wing is severely crippled.

The Constellation crashes and burns about 1,000 feet up from the Colorado River, at the mouth of the Grand Canyon. Aboard the DC-7, there is pandemonium. Those not wearing their seat belts are flung into the air as the plane careens. The captain screams his last words into the radio: "We're going in!"

Is Kate thinking, *I'm not supposed to be here—it's not my time?*

Near the confluence of the deep blue Little Colorado and the muddy Colorado stands Chuar Butte, a 3,700-foot-high pedestal of rock. The DC-7 hurtles toward the cliffs of red-hued limestone, striking with such force that about half of the wreckage scatters over the plateau. During the following week, army helicopter rescue crews will brave high winds and treacherous conditions to get to the remote crash site. They find only small pieces of the DC-7. Nothing recognizable has survived.

*

My Christmases are different than before. Sure, I buy presents for my wife and children, but I don't really care about receiving anything in return. I already have something that can't be shrink-wrapped or put on sale. It's that grace my dad was talking about. Grace—a funny word, not easy to define out of context. For me, it's the smell of coffee brewing. It's swimming in the icy waters of Willoughby Lake. It's swallowing the moon and watching the light shoot out from my fingertips. It's a passionate kiss I never want to end, that perfect moment in Beethoven's Ninth when the soloists are all by themselves, soaring. It's watching my children sleep.

I was raised a Unitarian. You've probably heard the joke: What do you get when you cross a Jehovah's Witness with a Unitarian? Answer: Someone who knocks on your door for no particular reason. I tend to think that there are rational explanations for things that happen in nature. And that whatever science doesn't explain now, it probably will in the future.

Kate was, I believe, the Accidental Guardian. Still, it is not a huge leap of my imagination to think that something happened that day back in June of 1956. Amid the chaos, the Grand Canyon echoed with terrible sounds, from the rumble of thunder to the wail of bending metal, to the final horrific boom of exploding fuel. And yet, above all these sounds, simple and clear, there was the ringing of a solitary bell.

My dad—always the engineer—has a more grounded view. After we had trudged down the mountain he turned and smiled at John and me. He said, "And the moral of the story is: If someone asks you for a favor, *do it*."

ABOUT THE AUTHOR

Ted Page is a storyteller and performer. His nonfiction stories have appeared in *Boston* magazine and the *Boston Globe Magazine*, and his comedy screen credits include work with John Cleese and Florence Henderson. While Ted's professional life as the co-founder of Captains of Industry (a marketing firm) has led him to projects with legends of the entertainment industry, it is his true stories about his family that have resonated most with audiences. As a member of the Souled Out Artists group, Ted performed many of the stories from his book, *The Willoughby Chronicles*, polishing them over a five-year period based on audience feedback. Ted has two children, two grandsons, one wife and two cats, not listed here in order of importance.

CPSIA information can be obtained
at www.ICGtesting.com
Printed in the USA
BVOW03s0817290917
496291BV00001B/11/P